I'M NOT HOLDING YOUR COAT

MY *BRUISES-AND-ALL*
MEMOIR OF
PUNK ROCK *REBELLION*

NANCY BARILE

Bazillion
Points

D0514792

I'M NOT HOLDING YOUR COAT
My Bruises-and-All Memoir of Punk Rock Rebellion

Second printing, published in 2021 by

Bazillion Points
New York | New York
United States
bazillionpoints.com

ISBN 978-1-935950-20-2
Printed in the United States

Cover layout and design by Bazillion Points
Cover concept by Lisa Haun; cover photo by Rikki Ercoli
Produced by Ian Christe
Edited by Polly Watson

A bazillion thanks to Al Barile, Tony Rettman, Lisa Haun, Mike Gitter,
Bryan Lathrop, Allison Schnackenberg, Dianna, Vivienne, and Roman.

Library of Congress Control Number: 2020948347
Library of Congress Cataloging-in-Publication Data is available upon request.

Previous overleaf: *My friends told me about the Bad Brains, but I had to witness them myself.*
This is me the first time I saw the Bad Brains at the Elks Center, January 1982. The look on my
face says it all. PHOTO BY KAREN KOUMJIAN

For my parents, Millie and Sam,
who didn't know any of this was happening,
but who always trusted me to
do the right thing

RIKKI ERCOLI

TABLE OF CONTENTS

A CONVERSATION WITH IAN MACKAYE

My husband, SSD guitarist Al Barile, introduced me to Ian MacKaye, front man of Minor Threat (and eventually Fugazi) and founder of Dischord Records, in September 1982. Our shared experiences brought us together, and I came to respect Ian as a visionary, archivist, musician, and friend. Ian is true-blue, and I can't say that about a lot of people. I started this project to add a woman's voice to a history that seemed to be erasing it. But this story is about more than that, and I looked to Ian to help me frame why was I still talking about punk and hardcore after so many years. I visited Dischord House outside Washington, DC, to speak with Ian and gain perspective on why the music and the scene associated with early-1980s hardcore continue to remain so important to so many of us. The following are his replies in our conversation.

ONE OF THE PROBLEMS WITH THE HISTORICAL NATURE OF PUNK ROCK is that when people talk about the punk scene, they tend to base what they're saying on available images. Therefore, descriptions of the early days are almost always going to focus on the bands, because that's where the cameras were pointing. But those bands were just the people creating the music, and I think music largely acts as a form of currency for specific communities. The three or four people on the stage were not solely indicative of the scene— they were creating the currency of the scene at that moment. The real scene could be found sitting on the curb outside of the venue. It was boys and girls and men and women.

The tendency people have to think that the early American punk scene was just all a bunch of young boys, and white boys, is factually incorrect. When I think back about "the scene," I rarely think about the bands. I mostly think about sitting out front of the 9:30 Club after the gig, or going to meet up with people at Ikaros Pizza, or just walking around Georgetown looking for friends. People obviously didn't have cell phones in the late '70s and early '80s. When we got out of school and we wanted to see our friends, there was no way to call them. To find anyone, we just went to wherever people hung out. There were a couple of record shops and ice cream spots in Georgetown that one might check, but all you really needed to do was walk around, because eventually you would run into another punk. Then you would start walking with them and before too long someone else would show up, and there would be three of you, and so on. That's just the way the gathering worked, and it was a boys-and-girls thing, not just boys.

Nancy has written a book about her time being a punk in Philly in the early 1980s, when the hardcore punk scene was this incredible tribal unfolding. The American punk scene in the early 1980s—the American punk underground at that time—was especially significant because it was one of the first times that kids, young people, decided to start their own bands, put on their own shows, publish their own fanzines, and create their own labels to put out their own records completely outside of the music industry. The punk thing for me, and I imagine for most of us, was a way to find a connection, because, for a variety of reasons, we felt marginalized in society. We used music as a gathering point or a currency or a secret language, and this made it possible to more easily spot a fellow traveler. It was entirely possible to spot someone on the street, and *know* that they knew that you both knew something special.

My sense is that a lot of people who have decided to write about punk, or make documentaries on the subject, tend to focus on the more sensational aspects of the history. It makes for an easier story to tell. If someone went to a party where there were thirty people in a room, twenty-eight of those people could be engaged in fascinating conversations. But if two got into a fistfight, that conflict would probably be the report of the evening. I reckon this is a result of our society's fascination with violence. I think when people start telling stories about the scene, the reason they so often talk about fights and craziness is because those are the more dramatic moments. Those are the things we remember. You remember being chased down the street by thugs, or the cops shutting down a show.

Though the Camden, New Jersey, show that Nancy and others promoted in 1982 was an epic evening filled with interactions, my central memory is of getting hit by a car. Those are dramatic things, but more notably, they're things that appear on the surface of an era that is so important to us that we are still talking about it decades later. Maybe they serve as something akin to mile markers along the road of life. I can easily recall getting hit by that car, but that didn't lead to my sense of a tribal connection—it was the fact that it occurred within the long arc of the punk hang that really cemented the relationship with fellow punks. I reckon it's really the more mundane day-in and day-out of the scene that became so important to me. Those "highlights" are just ways to tell stories that direct us back toward this sense of family, which I think, ultimately, was what punk really was for me, and, I suspect, a lot of other people.

Really, in my mind, the hardships that people talk about are really just indicators. For instance, when you hear stories from elders about having to walk through the snow to get to school, what's important isn't the walk. It's the school. And that's the way that I look at the punk scene. When I read books in which people are talking about all the crazy stuff that was going on, I think what they're really trying to communicate is that it was a time so important to us that we put up with the madness.

—*Ian MacKaye, July 6, 2018*

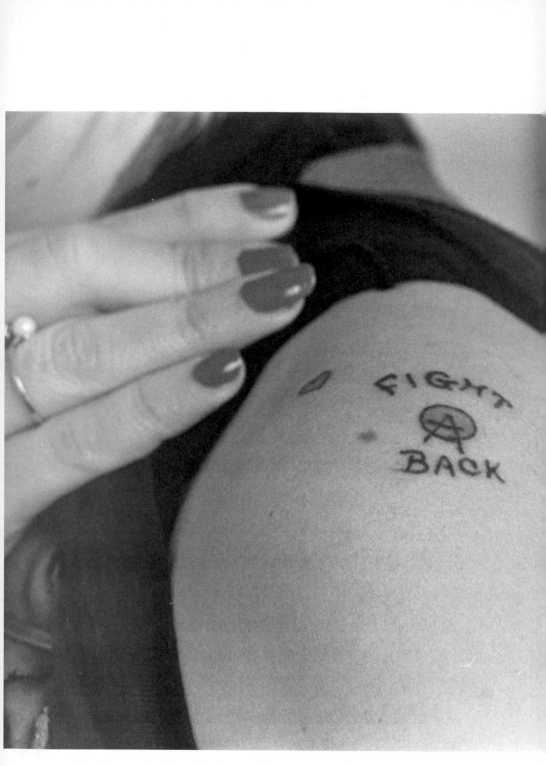

In 1981, not a lot of people had tattoos, but I went one night and got the anarchy "A".
(I know, I know, but it was 1981!) And because I worshipped Discharge, and I always felt
like I was fighting someone or something, I added "Fight Back." GAIL RUSH

INTRODUCTION

"**I FOUND YOUR PICTURE ON THE INTERNET LAST NIGHT,**" smirked John, a student in my AP Literature class. "You were a punk rocker! In the picture, you have dyed-blonde hair, and you're wearing a leather jacket. You're with a girl with pink hair, who is totally out of it. Look, I printed it out!" He waved the photo above his head.

I felt the blood rush to my face. I knew that some of my students were aware that I had once been involved in a music scene. But for fifteen years, I had kept the depth of my involvement with punk rock a professional secret. As an educator, I didn't think black eyes and stage diving would play well with parents or administrators. But as the internet filled up with historical documents from the dawn of hardcore punk, my past life in the early 1980s was increasingly only a Google search away. Now I was on the spot, and I had to decide quickly how to reckon with my punk rock past.

I glanced at the photo while my students all craned their necks for a glimpse. There I was in 1981 with my best friend, Allison Schnackenberg, backstage at CBGB, the notorious punk club on the Bowery in New York City. The walls were splattered with colorful graffiti. My white-blonde hair was short and streaked with a vein of bright blue. I was wearing a jacket—the only coat I ever held for anyone—that I had saved up for months to have custom-made by an old leather craftsman in Philly. The names of my favorite bands were written all over it in white marker. Underneath, I wore a silky lace camisole and rosary beads—a pre-Madonna look I'd co-opted from the Puerto Rican messengers I worked with at a law firm, where I was a word processor.

"Oh, I remember this picture." I smiled. "That was one of the best days of my life."

I laughed as my students barraged me with questions about my punk rock days. Since that episode, my life has been an open book to the kids. Punk rock, I realize, has actually helped me become a better teacher in ways that I didn't understand at the beginning of my career. As the years pass, I appreciate my punk roots more and more.

Going from punk rock to teaching is probably not a common trajectory, but my path is integral to my being the teacher I am. Over more than twenty-five years now as an educator, I've won several awards for teaching, and I have often been asked what training and education provided me with the skills necessary to be effective. When I moved beyond the simple rote answers and thought about it deeply, I realized that—despite years of schooling, multiple degrees, and countless hours of professional development—punk rock contributed much more to my ability to connect with my students and help them than any teacher training program.

Through punk rock, I was able to understand and reach disenfranchised and marginalized teens—mainly because I was one, and so were my friends. As a teacher, I don't want to leave my students stranded in the classroom, ignored by disinterested and unenthusiastic teachers the way I was when I was in school. I want to forge bonds and relationships that empower my students and help them take ownership of their school and their learning.

Punk enabled me to recognize the importance of self-expression through language. As a teacher, I encourage my students to tap into the power of words to communicate rage and bliss, and, of course, to make a difference in the world. Back then, we self-published xeroxed fanzines that reflected our thoughts on politics, social issues, and, especially, music. That act of sharing our perspective changed us. In 2012 when my students Will, Rawlings, Jose, and Alfredo told me about the struggles they faced in school as young men of color, I urged them to speak out and tell their stories. The College Board published their essays, and the boys went on to take part in a national webinar and to lead a session at a College Board regional forum. In speaking up, they made an impact that they'd never dreamed possible. Now, more than ever, it's important for young people to have their voices heard.

Most punks I met in the late 1970s and early 1980s were good, socially conscious people. Even today, it's interesting to see that so many of my contemporaries embrace the same ideas and beliefs about life that I do. I believe our attitudes, our philosophies, and our do-it-yourself work ethic were all the result of the generation we were born into and the music scene we adopted. So many of those who were involved in this music scene became lifelong educators, activists, organizers, environmentalists, volunteers, and ethical business owners.

I feel strongly that our punk roots made our aspirations a natural outgrowth of what we went through as kids. I often wish more people shared our experiences so that the impact would be larger, wider, and even more intense. We were bound together by the bands and, in many cases, the politics. The times necessitated that we become superb communicators. We made crazy expensive long-distance phone calls and wrote epic letters delivered by the US Postal Service because we realized that communication was vital. We talked about new and upcoming bands; we talked about mutual friends. We set up shows and shared content for fanzines. The ability to cover great distances and tear down walls through communication became a powerful asset in my teaching career.

Punk rock introduced me to a diverse and multicultural world. It taught me to believe in the strength of music and the arts to break down racial, ethnic, and class barriers and unite people. The punk creed I subscribed to railed against racism, prejudice, and hatred of any kind. Now, as a teacher, I often create assignments that ask my students to take a stand despite conflicting data, complicated politics, and intense societal pressure. I want to equip my students with the skills necessary to understand perspectives and cultures and to comprehend, critique, and demonstrate independence. My students are constantly being bombarded with information on social media, and so much of it is untrue. I want to prepare them for this world so they can evaluate sources and make informed decisions without being swayed by someone else's bias.

The do-it-yourself work ethic, so vital to the punk rock scene in the early '80s, has proven immensely valuable to me in gaining resources, knocking down walls, and refusing to take no for an answer when it comes to my students. And that sets a strong example. Back in the early 1980s, when I realized that I couldn't see the bands I loved because they weren't playing huge stadium venues, or they were only booked into nightclubs I wasn't old enough to enter, I took matters into my own hands. I rented Elks centers and Knights of Columbus halls, and I called bands from all over the world to come and play shows. That's how I met my husband, Al Barile. He and his band SSD were busy spreading the word about the straight edge movement, the anti-drug and anti-drinking culture that lives on today.

Punk taught me to not be manipulated for the sake of a personal agenda, especially if I believe it will harm my students. Even at this age, I continue to question authority; my stance still gets me into trouble from time to time. But I refuse to blindly follow the directives of leaders who attempt to compromise my integrity or the integrity of those kids I'm entrusted to help.

In my classroom, punk rock lives.

With Allison Schnackenberg at CBGB in 1981. COURTESY OF ALLISON SCHNACKENBERG
Overleaf: *In a gritty alley that I loved near my Philadelphia apartment.* RIKKI ERCOLI

See, I am a natural blonde! Clockwise from top left: *With my dad and brother Danny at the U.S. Capitol. I insisted on wearing loafers exactly like my dad's. After a few hours of sightseeing, my feet were bloody, but I didn't say a word!; Eleven years old with Danny and my beagle Mickey; Our family swim club, still a common Philadelphia thing. At left is the "dance area" where we would play the jukebox and dance on hot summer days.*

OLD SCHOOL

WHEN I WAS ELEVEN, THE SCARIEST THING IN THE WORLD to me was a Catholic-school nun. Nuns and priests ruled the classrooms of the 1960s with an iron fist while clutching rosary beads. Students did what they were told or faced the wrath of a system that did not hear or respect their voices.

St. Titus was a newly built school in Norristown, Pennsylvania. The building's façade reflected the current 1970s style of architecture with clean lines and sleek crosses. School there began before construction finished, so the school was lacking a library, a complete cafeteria, and a gym. But Titus was modern compared to other grade schools in the area, and the classrooms were spacious and clean.

My school career didn't start out so badly. In first grade, I adored my teacher, Sister Regina Anthony. She smelled like Revlon Jean Naté cologne, and she was soft-spoken and kind. We knew she cared about us. She spoke sweetly to every student, even those who could be mischievous in class, and she had infinite patience.

I'm not sure why she singled me out, but one day she tapped me gently on the shoulder and said: "Nancy Petriello, come here. I want you to read this book to me." I started to tremble, terrified that I was in trouble. I stumbled over some of the words, but I knew most of them. I was frightened but at the same time excited. I realized that what was happening was good. Significantly, I can picture the moment vividly fifty-five years later.

My mother taught me to read at an early age, and books were an important part of our household. Both my parents were voracious readers: my mother read thick historical novels that took two hands to carry, and my father read fiction by Ken Follett and Willard Motley, as well as nonfiction books on war, political science, and US and global history. Trips to the bookmobile were as exciting as a night at the drive-in movie theater. In fact, my mother often had to convince the bookmobile librarian to let me take out more books than children were permitted. The bookmobile only came to our area once a month, and I would often finish my books the first week.

At the end of the school day after reading to the class, Sister Regina Anthony tucked a note into my book bag. She said, "I want you to give this note to your parents when you get home, okay?"

I had seen Sister give notes to misbehaving boys. My heart raced, and I felt sick to my stomach, petrified that I had done something wrong. I waited until after dinner to quietly hand the note to my mother as she sat alone at the kitchen table. I definitely did not want my dad to see it. I watched my mom's face as she read it, and I was so relieved when her face broke into a wide grin.

"Sister says you have advanced reading skills," my mother told me. "She's going to give you some books that will be a little more challenging for you to read in class." My mother was thrilled by the news. I'm sure if I went through the drawers of my childhood home today, I would find that letter stuffed in a Bible or wedged in a cubbyhole somewhere because it made my mother so happy.

After that, Sister pulled me aside each day for my own reading lesson, and she sent books home with me every week. I cherished that special treatment, and I worked hard to continue to earn her respect and praise— not just in reading, but in all my subjects. I tried not to be chatty with my friends or be off task. I offered to clean the blackboards and clap erasers—

highly coveted jobs in our class—and was thrilled when I was frequently chosen to carry out those tasks.

My joyful experiences in Sister Regina Anthony's class basically continued from second through fifth grades. I loved school. My teachers were competent and compassionate. I looked up to them and sought their approval. During vacations, I missed going to school, and I was anxious to return. But in sixth grade, all that changed.

In sixth grade, I met Sister Alice. A little gnome of a woman, Sister Alice stood about four and a half feet tall. She was, and remains to this day, one of the meanest people I have ever met. Suddenly, the very embodiment of every wicked witch and evil stepmother I had read about in books was now sitting, facing me, at the teacher's desk in my classroom.

Sister Alice took great delight in embarrassing and humiliating her students. "Stand up!" she screamed at Kathy, a shy girl who cried easily. In Catholic school, students always had to stand up when addressed or when answering a question; the practice was anxiety-inducing, especially for timid students. She berated Kathy until Kathy broke down sobbing.

Sister Alice was especially vicious to the boys in the class. She shrieked at them, "Get your hands out of your pockets! I know what you're doing in there!" Or: "You're stupid! You're lazy! You're dumb!" She provoked them into retaliating, just so she could throw them out of class or further shame them.

When Sister Alice asked for students to come in early to clean the classroom and dust the statues of the Blessed Mother and Jesus on her desk, my friend Maria and I volunteered. But she hit us with the rags and yelled, "You're not opening the cloth properly! You stupid child, you have no idea what you're doing!" Sometimes when I'm cleaning my own home, I still hear her screaming at me: "Open the cloth first and then fold it over!" It was well into the school year before Sister Alice even knew my name—or the names of any of her students. Before long, I dreaded going to school. All my friends felt the same way.

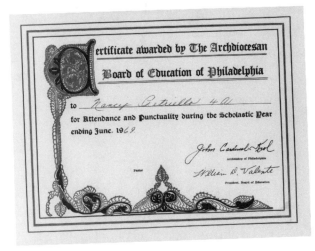

Putting the "punk" in punctuality in elementary school. In the beginning, I loved learning.

Mathias was probably the brightest student in our class, especially in math and science. He lived right next to the school, and one night, his house caught fire. In school the next day, we smelled the acrid smoke and saw the charred remains of his home through our classroom windows. Despite this, Mattie still came to class that morning, dressed in jeans and a polo shirt. Sister Alice, who surely knew his situation as we all did, screeched: "Where is your uniform? How dare you come to class without your uniform on!" Mattie hung his head in shame, too fearful to try to defend himself.

Sister Alice never left her desk during class. She taught the same grammar lessons over and over. Art and music were canceled. Students spent the year cowering in terror. I think I must have spent my two remaining years of grammar school recovering from genuine post-traumatic stress disorder.

My friends and I *still* share stories of Sister Alice's cruelty and bullying. But that woman played an important part in the formation of my rebellious identity, inspiring my fledgling move away from authority. She primed me to be a punk. For the first time, a symbol of authority was clearly the enemy. That concept was difficult for my obedient-young-Catholic-schoolgirl brain to process at first. Unfortunately, she was the first of several abusive, incompetent teachers and authority figures I met in Catholic school. One by one, they caused my rebellion to build, making a long-lasting impact on my life and later informing my adult career as a teacher.

Just when I sorely needed it, a new television show debuted called *Room 222*. The comedy-drama was set in a high school in Los Angeles, particularly an American history class taught by a character named Mr. Dixon. One of the coolest people on TV, the fictional Mr. Dixon was tuned into what was important to his students. He was a great listener in and out of the classroom. While multicultural Walt Whitman High was about as far away as you could get from my private school in a mostly white suburb of Philadelphia, I connected strongly with the program. I couldn't wait to turn on the TV to watch a new episode every Friday night.

Room 222 reflected the political and social climate of the early 1970s. The students in Mr. Dixon's classes wore huge Afros, miniskirts, and love beads. These teenagers were insightful and intelligent, and their class discussions were *deep*. In different episodes they worked through their issues with the Vietnam War, domestic violence, drug abuse, gay rights, and women's rights. In Mr. Dixon's class, students didn't raise their hands for permission to talk. They listened to one another, and they respected each other's opinions. Most importantly, it was clear that student voices and opinions were valued in Mr. Dixon's classroom.

Riding the bus to school, I asked my best friend, Andrea, "Why can't our school be like *Room 222*? Why can't we take on the world's problems the way they do in Mr. Dixon's class?"

"Forget it, Nancy," Andrea replied. "It's not going to happen at St. Titus."

Instead of having an involved guidance counselor or a beleaguered, cranky, yet totally compassionate principal who truly looked out for his students, we were stuck with Sister Alice, who stifled creativity and replaced it with conformity. Even for a rare creative writing assignment, Sister Alice had one way of doing things—her way. Nothing else was acceptable. She rambled on about the dangers of sex and the "pollution" of television.

Don't let the uniforms fool you—a rebellion was simmering.

She repeated herself daily and ranted about the Russians corrupting youth through rock and roll.

Of course, looking back, I realize Sister Alice was most likely in the early stages of dementia as a result of her advanced age. She must have been somewhere in her seventies, based on her memories of Grover Cleveland. But no principal, parent, teacher, or nun ever intervened or tried to stop her abuse. No one stepped in to help. Most parents in the 1960s deferred to the authority of teachers. If I went home and told my mother and father about Sister Alice's mistreatment of us, I was certain they would blame me and believe we kids had gotten what we deserved.

It didn't help that my father, a former Marine, ruled our household with a strict and sometimes physical hand. A test that came home with a grade of 95 would be condemned because it wasn't a 100. Coming home a minute late, not refilling the water pitcher in the refrigerator, or dropping something often resulted in a backhand to the face. Complaining about a nun would probably have brought a quick dose of the same. So I busied myself with cheerleading and Girl Scouts, while my love of learning was sorely curtailed. Instead of diving into my education, I rebelled. And what better time for rebellion than the early 1970s?

I don't believe it was a coincidence that my first act of defiance came in sixth grade. Each morning, as the buses arrived at school, students were forced to wait outside on the "playground," the term a misnomer for a patch of concrete that was nothing more than a huge parking lot. We were never permitted to wait inside the school. Since my bus was one of the first to arrive, I often stayed outside for an hour or more—whether in the cold, rain, or snow. Most of us hated it. On winter mornings, it took almost an hour for my icy fingers to thaw out before I could write a word in class. No one wanted to play schoolyard games like red rover or practice cheerleading in that weather. I longed to be inside, where I could at least read or do homework.

I decided to start a petition. I worked that playground like a Vietnam War protester, gathering signatures from nearly every student in the school. After two weeks, I presented the petition to the principal of the school, Sister Pius. She was appalled.

"You need to offer up your discomfort from the elements to God!" she told me.

Sister Pius brought in Father Pope, the pastor who ran the parish, adding more terror to the situation. He glowered at me. "How dare you question our authority!"

I was given no opportunity to explain or defend my position. And despite having the facts, evidence, and rationales I needed, I was too scared to open my mouth. "Talking back" was just not done.

"You are incorrigible and insubordinate," they screamed, while I stood there trembling. I wasn't even sure what those words meant, but I knew they weren't complimentary.

After a few days, however, we learned that the administration had finally agreed to let students wait inside the building after the morning bus drop-off. Despite getting in trouble in school and later at home, I rejoiced at what I considered a significant victory. My classmates looked at me proudly, and I felt we had won the fight together. Their signatures could not be ignored—the people had prevailed. I couldn't openly celebrate; my parents were far too angry at being contacted by the school. But at night in bed, I played the scene over and over in my head. Being yelled at had been scary, but the success was definitely worth it. Rebellion tasted good. I had fought the man and won.

INTRO TO JUKEBOX

I **WAS FIVE IN 1964**, when I was first able to use the record player by myself. I played my Beatles, Dave Clark Five, and Chubby Checker forty-fives over and over. My dad took my brother, sister, and me to Babe's Luncheonette on Main Street in Norristown on the outskirts of Philadelphia, where we ordered huge "zep" submarine sandwiches and milkshakes and played the jukebox. A quarter was worth three songs. I played Roger Miller's "King of the Road" every single time. To this day, I remember another favorite choice, "Mony Mony" by Tommy James and the Shondells, was mechanical push-button selection number E3.

Riding in the car one day, I heard a song called "The House of the Rising Sun" by the Animals. Shivers shot down my spine. Even at five years old, I felt attuned to the darker, more dangerous kind of music out there. Eric Burdon's vocals were gritty and uncompromising, as he sang, "It's been the ruin of many a poor boy, and, God, I know I'm one."

I couldn't help noticing that my mother *always* changed the station whenever that song came on the radio. When I got my own transistor radio for Christmas in 1964, I'd listen to WFIL 560 AM constantly, waiting to hear "House of the Rising Sun." Whenever it played, I would sing along in my head, secretly.

Like most families in America, we watched *The Ed Sullivan Show* every Sunday night. I screamed along with every other kid when the Beatles performed, but the first time I saw the Rolling Stones on the show, I knew there was something a bit more threatening—and alluring—about them. My young mind couldn't process why. But again, my mom disproved of their performance. I loved it.

So many songs I heard all around me in the '60s and '70s caused me to think deeply about the world with lyrics about protest and revolution. When I was eight, my sister, Jeanne, who was two years older, used to sing Dion's "Abraham, Martin and John" to me when I was restless and couldn't sleep. I knew from school that those men had been assassinated. I discovered that I liked that kind of socially conscious songwriting. "Abraham, Martin and John" was a stark contrast to, say, the Archies' "Sugar, Sugar" which, let's face it, *was* an amazing tune but didn't keep me up at night questioning the meaning of life.

By the early 1970s, the turmoil of the world beyond my life was hard to ignore. The Vietnam War was raging; planes were being hijacked; the Manson family murders had brought a well-publicized trial; and in 1972 even the Munich Olympics became the scene of a massacre.

The Crosby, Stills, Nash & Young song "Ohio" scared me. I asked my mom, "What is this song about?" She told me what had happened at Kent State. I was eleven years old, and hearing that the National Guard had killed unarmed college students freaked me out, causing more sleepless nights.

I realized there was a great deal wrong with the world, and I felt a tug of responsibility to change things. I was starting to understand the true power of music, and, as a rebellious kid coming of age, I felt the deep connection between music and social causes that would become an important part of my life.

No wonder so many of us who grew up during this time turned to punk rock in the late '70s and early '80s. The music of our early youth built a significant foundation and had a long-lasting and powerful effect. I appreciate that the pop music of the '70s could just as easily feature an earworm like Starland Vocal Band's "Afternoon Delight" as the protest song "Hurricane" by Bob Dylan, about boxer Rubin Carter. Intense, thought-provoking, and socially conscious songs like the Temptations' "Ball of Confusion" and Marvin Gaye's "What's Going On?" were mixed in with novelty fare like Captain & Tenille's "Muskrat Love." Hearing these anthems of rebellion, change, and protest played on commercial radio had a profound effect on my musical development, as well as my moral development. The music built on lessons implanted in me as a Catholic elementary school girl, which no longer felt sufficient.

My family was fortunate enough to belong to a swim club, which had a jukebox and a dance area. Preteens and teenagers gathered inside, listening to tunes and dancing to the Jackson 5's "The Love You Save," Rare Earth's version of "(I Know) I'm Losing You," the Rolling Stones' "Honky Tonk Women," and Led Zeppelin's "Trampled Under Foot." My absolute favorite dance song was, and remains, "Fire" by the Ohio Players. My mom would come over to the dance area, wearing her clip-on sunglasses and straw sun hat, and shake her head. "It's ninety-eight degrees!" she'd complain. "Stop hanging out in there and get into the pool!"

Needless to say, just like the more-celebrated radio, the jukebox had a huge impact on kids in the 1970s. Jukeboxes were very cool for reasons unique to the format. They made a wide variety of music accessible to us. Sharing music we loved—and learned to love—in a public place became an act of identity. For us as young people starting to figure out who we were and *what* we were, music was one of the first identifiers of personality. The music we chose predicted our group identity. Being able to represent that in a public setting alongside both peers and parents was a big step toward finding one's true self. It was like planting your flag and declaring loudly, "Here I am. This is who I am and who I will be, and this is the music I've chosen that best represents that."

I sat on the railing of the dance area and waited. When my turn came, I'd push in my dime and select K5 to play Bad Company's "Can't Get Enough," or L8 to hear David Bowie's "Space Oddity," and people would learn a little about me. Then when I next keyed up Sly and the Family Stone or the Isley Brothers, I was adding a bit more to the calculus. Meanwhile, I was building the same personality profiles in my head for anyone else choosing their songs. Unlike the Walkman, which came later, or even the transistor radio, the jukebox was a public expression of who you were and what you were into.

❦

I entered Bishop Kenrick High School in 1973 at the age of fourteen. Just like in grade school, I faced more incompetent and ineffective adults— teachers who clearly did not see their career as a chance to educate and enlighten students. Even as a fourteen-year-old, I could easily recognize that many of my teachers were not qualified to teach their courses. The nun who taught algebra was near deaf and had a hard time communicating. Kids tormented her by mouthing words or slamming books. My Spanish teacher was ancient and never moved beyond the first chapters of the book. My Business English teacher didn't know the difference between *its* and *it's*.

Once again, many of these grown-ups were bullies. In social studies, a teacher made a boy stand for almost twenty minutes, while the teacher repeatedly asked a question to which the boy clearly did not know the answer. Another social studies teacher, this one also a football coach, made my friend Maria kneel on the floor in front of him because she was talking in class. I can think of no situation where it is appropriate for a teacher, particularly an adult man, to make a teenage girl kneel on the floor.

Such episodes are indicative of what went on in high school classrooms then, and not just at our school. Public humiliation was the norm. I didn't feel like I was learning much.

So I was shocked to find the one thing my conservative Catholic high school *did* have: a jukebox in the cafeteria. I walked into our lunchroom as a terrified freshman and heard David Essex's "Rock On" on the jukebox, and felt at ease for the first time. Glam rock was in full swing that year, reflected not only in the music but also in the clothes we wore. The girls sported platform shoes and glittery socks with their school uniforms. The boys wore silky satin dress shirts and long hair. I crushed on those cool boys every single day of high school.

At the start of my freshman year of high school, my sister, now a junior, moved out of our shared bedroom and into the basement for more privacy. She bought a stereo, and every day after school she played her albums for hours. Music drifted up through the floorboards. When she wasn't home, I would sneak down to the basement to try to figure out which records I liked. The J. Geils Band and Foghat I didn't like so much. Those records sounded like what I already heard on the radio. But David Bowie, Lou Reed, T. Rex, and Mott the Hoople were a giant, fresh, and appealing *yes*!

I got a cassette tape recorder that Christmas. When my sister was at work, I taped all my favorite albums: Bowie's *Hunky Dory*, *Ziggy Stardust*, *Pinups*, and *Aladdin Sane*; T. Rex's *Electric Warrior* and *The Slider*; and Lou Reed's *Rock N Roll Animal*. I had to be stealthy, and the secret operation took days and days. But soon I had my own collection of music to listen to whenever I wanted. Of course, I would still sneak downstairs to pore over the album covers, lyric sheets, and liner notes.

Everything about David Bowie intrigued me. His music was deeper and more moving than the rest of what was being played on AM radio. Somehow, he reached into my soul—like he was singing directly to me. I listened to Bowie's records repeatedly and memorized the lyrics; I was desperate to see him perform. I stared at his albums for hours. Bowie was unlike anyone I had ever heard or seen before. His voice was smoothly beautiful, and his lyrics were evocative and mysterious to my fourteen-year-old self. I remember my little brother, Danny, who was ten at the time, crying when I told him what "Space Oddity" was about. "Wait," he wailed. "You mean he *never* gets back to Earth?"

The only way we kids could see live music performances was by staying up late to watch *The Midnight Special* or *Don Kirshner's Rock Concert*. My parents didn't allow us stay up late for those, but I had a babysitting gig that enabled me to watch those shows frequently. I took as many babysitting jobs as I could, not just for the money, but also for access to the bands I loved and to see and learn about new ones.

When I found out Bowie's *1980 Floor Show* was going to be aired on *The Midnight Special* on a non-babysitting night, I had to corner my mom. "Please, can I stay up and watch Bowie?" I begged. She acquiesced, and actually watched the show with my sister and me, probably to monitor something so troubling that it could only be broadcast on television late at night. I know a part of her was freaked out, but there was a larger part of her that was as enthralled. To my complete surprise, she became an instant fan, and loved Bowie as much as I did. "He's weird, but there *is* something about him," she said.

Watching Bowie perform live solidified my lasting love for him. I wanted everyone to know how awesome he was. When I was assigned a project for religion class my freshman year, my friend Andrea and I created a presentation with photos and pictures and set the entire production to the songs "Five Years" and "Changes." Our teacher Sister Donna Michelle was very hip and cool, especially for a nun. She loved our project. For Arts Day, she arranged for us to go around and do our presentation for other classes, including the upperclassmen. We were thrilled.

❧

I was anxious to discover the whole wide world of music on FM radio and albums. I started to hang out in the record stores at the Plymouth Meeting Mall. I talked to the salespeople behind the counter, usually guys with an encyclopedic knowledge of music. They turned me on to records by Kraftwerk and Brian Eno. "If you're not listening to Brian Eno's *Taking Tiger Mountain (by Strategy)*," one young salesman told me, "you're not really listening to music."

I bought the Eno record immediately and listened to it incessantly. "Can you please, please, please listen to something else?" my mother begged. I also became obsessed with Bowie's Spiders from Mars guitarist, Mick Ronson, and his records got me through some oppressive times in high school.

High school and the world around me often made me angry and discouraged. My sense of fairness was bothered when people were treated differently because they weren't wearing the same Bass Weejuns or Peters jackets everyone else was wearing. I was frustrated by the rampant conformity and lack of creativity in high school. And I felt unable to change any of the horrors I saw daily on TV: wars, hijackings, kidnappings, crime, brutal government authority, poverty, and injustice. I wanted to *do something*, but I was unequipped and uninformed. And I wasn't learning anything in school that would empower me.

In my early years of high school, I participated in school activities and tried to take ownership of my school. I took advantage of working with the system as best I could. I was elected to student council, and I joined several clubs. Like many adolescent girls, after watching amazing Soviet gymnast Olga Korbut rack up gold medals during the 1972 Olympics, I started gymnastics. I was a tentative tumbler, though, and the male coach quickly crushed any dreams of Olympic fame. He wasn't willing to work with someone who was just learning the sport. Even more discouraging, I realized that the students at my school had no real power and that every new idea or progressive thought would be squashed; I reluctantly quit the student council.

Favoritism was rampant. It aggravated me to see the special treatment awarded the male jocks and what we called the "rah-rahs." These kids had *way* too much school spirit, and were *way* too invested in the outcome of Friday night's game. Once my friend Rich and I were caught listening to Lou Reed, T. Rex, and David Bowie in the library, instead of foreign language tapes. We were both busted. I received ten demerits and detention. Rich, a football player, received no punishment at all. After that, I was done trying to conform to my high school's social hierarchy. I wanted to do my own thing. I wasn't quite sure what my own thing was, but I knew there had to be more to life than boring lectures, irrelevant classwork, stifling conformity, and Friday night football games.

The one activity I continued was contributing to the music section of the school paper. I enjoyed writing concert and album reviews, and I was able to share my love of music with a wider audience.

I listened to music as an escape from a stifling, patriarchal household and a bleak educational environment. Music had always been a big part of my life, but now I began to recognize that it had the power to take me out of my suffocating surroundings and give me a voice where before I'd had none. By the end of freshman year, I was ready for a big change.

Green and gold spirit day at my high school, so of course I dressed all in black. That's me at far left in the offending transition lens glasses. And I sure was going through a transition.

Rod Stewart
1. Alice Cooper-Suzi Quatro
2. Kiss - Ted Nugent
3. Roxy Music
4. Sparks, Mott, UFO
5. Frampton - Gary Wright
6. Super-tramp - Ace
7. Kiss
8. Patti Smith- Johnny's Dance Band
9. Nils Lofgren-E. Murphy, S Gibbons
10. David Bowie
11. The Tubes- Thin Lizzie
12. McCartney. Wings
13. Nektar, E. Slick, Pavlovs Dog
14. Yes, Frampton, G. Wright, Pousette D.B.
15. Gentle Giant, Starcastle
16. Aerosmith - Derringer
17. Jefferson Starship-Sea Level
18. Nils Lofgren - Striders
19. Blue Oyster Cult- Manfred Mann
   Ansel

electric factory concerts
Eighteenth & Lombard Streets, Philadelphia.

21. Bruce Springsteen
22. Lou Reed
23. Manfred Mann-Canyon
24. Al Stewart
25. Hall and Oates-R Supa
26. Robert Palmer-Southside Johnny-G. Parker
27. Manhatten Transfer
28. Patti Smith - Sparks
29. Derringer-Slim Pickens
30. Kiss - Bob Seger
31. Robert Palmer-Striders
32. Queen-Thin Lizzie
33. Al Stewart - Wendy Wildmen
34. Iggy Pop (bowie) Blondie
35. Manfred Mann J. Miles
36. Ramones-Kenn Kweder
37. M. Murphy-Buzzy Linhart
38. Bay City Rollers
39. Patti Smith
40. David Bowie
41. Karen Bihari
42. Devo - David Jo Hansen

43. Roxy Music - Robert (
44. Joe Jackson-Moon Mar
45. The Police-The Cramps-
46. The Knack. The Foo
47. B-52's - The Rattl
48. Talking Heads- Pearl I
49. The Normals
50. Johnny's Dance Band
51. Tom Petty + The Heart
   Fabulous Poodle
52. The Buzzcocks -The
53. George Thorogood- Al
54. The A's
55. George Thorogood
56. Cramps
57. Romantics - Shi
58. XTC - Fingerprint
59. the A's
60. Ramones
61. Wreckless Eric
62. Peter Galbrie
63. DEVO
64. PIL

During high school, I listed every concert that I saw in this noteboo[k]
—I wish I had written down venues and dates, as we[ll]

3
SURVIVING HIGH SCHOOL

DURING MY SOPHOMORE YEAR OF HIGH SCHOOL, I began dating a senior class football player named Gerry. We only met because we sat near each other in the cafeteria. At first, Gerry and I had a contentious relationship— he teased me, and I tried to aggravate him. But he usually made me laugh, and that was the way to my heart.

On our first date, Gerry took me to see Brian De Palma's glam rock horror comedy musical *Phantom of the Paradise*, which I loved. Gerry was so nervous that he locked the keys in his car—while the car was still running. After school Gerry would take me to Gino's Hamburgers or McDonald's, where we had long talks about our future hopes and dreams.

Most importantly, Gerry and I shared a love of music. He took me to my second live concert: Rod Stewart and the Faces' farewell tour at the Philly Civic Center. I had only witnessed a live performance once before: Sonny and Cher at the Valley Forge Music Fair back in sixth grade. Granted, that show was incredible in its own way, but it was *sedate* compared to a Rod Stewart concert.

The experience was nothing short of an epiphany. I was fascinated by the concertgoers, all decked out in velvet, satin, and huge platform shoes. I was in awe of people I saw there like Peter Dello Buono, who had graduated from my high school and now looked like a rock star himself with his Rod- like mane of hair, sky-high boots, and pastel blazer. By the time the real

Rod Stewart, dressed in his signature plaid scarves, took the stage and the orgasmic sound of electric guitars filled the room, I was hooked. I shivered with excitement throughout the entire performance. I knew this was where I was supposed to be.

My parents were not thrilled—either about letting me date *or* go to concerts. But they liked Gerry, and my mother regularly intervened with my father so we could go out alone together. I felt lucky that my mother and I were so close. She was easygoing and lighthearted. Even when I was a teen, we had a wonderful time, shopping at the mall or going out to lunch. My mom found pleasure in simple things like going for walks in nature or sitting at the kitchen table talking. She listened if I had a fight with my friends, and she frequently stepped in between my dad and me.

High on the list of things my mother would never have understood or approved was Alice Cooper's Welcome to My Nightmare tour, which Gerry and I went to see at the Spectrum. Alice's show was an incredible combination of rock, shock, and theater. The show explored the nightmare of a boy named Steven and featured a nine-foot Cyclops, skeletons dancing across the stage, and just the right number of giant spiders. In perfectly choreographed synchronicity, characters projected on a screen would jump off that screen and become live on the stage. The overall effect was creepy and macabre, making songs like "Billion Dollar Babies," "I'm Eighteen," and "Cold Ethyl" feel all the more powerful. I loved it.

Suzi Quatro opened up for Alice. Clad in a leather jumpsuit, Suzi was tiny but mighty. She rocked tough that night, playing straight-up hard rock and roll tinged with a bit of glam. She played an electric bass almost as big as she was, and I remember exclaiming to Gerry, "This is awesome!" Seeing a woman onstage playing an instrument and kicking ass was inspiring. I went home and cut and feathered my hair just like Suzi's. And I became obsessed with live music.

A few weeks later, we saw Kiss at the Tower Theater. Even in 1975, their live show was already impressive—they leapt into the air wearing sky-high platform boots, and Gene Simmons spat blood and breathed fire fifteen feet into the air. Gerry and I also saw the hauntingly beautiful Roxy Music, and then the quirky brother duo Sparks.

I thoroughly enjoyed taking the Sixty-Ninth Street high-speed line from Norristown to Upper Darby for a Tower Theater show. The excitement began with seeing all the cool people on the train. I was only fifteen, and most of the concertgoers were older and intriguing to me. After we arrived, we would stop at a store across the street from the Tower called the Balcony, which sold concert memorabilia, photos, funky clothing, and jewelry. I'd save my money so I could buy a rock photo or a band T-shirt.

❦

Gerry was my first real boyfriend, and I loved our time together. After the school year, he graduated and joined the army. We vowed to wait out his four years in the military. We began writing weekly, almost daily letters to each other, but I was only fifteen, far too young to stay in a committed, long-distance relationship. I was still in the high school cafeteria where we'd met, after all.

I desperately wanted to continue going to concerts, but without a reliable male chaperone my parents balked. My dad felt I was safe going to concerts in Philly when I had a man to protect me, but he wasn't willing to let me go on my own. Then I reconnected with Karen, a friend from school who shared my love of music.

Karen and I had both taken Sister Donna Michelle's religion class during our freshman year. Sister Donna Michelle was one of the best teachers at Bishop Kenrick, mainly because she used story structure to make religion relevant to fifteen-year-olds. Over the course of six months, Sister Donna Michelle told us the stories of Alfred Hitchcock's *Psycho*, the Who's rock opera *Tommy*, and William Friedkin's *The Exorcist*. Almost every day she left us with a cliffhanger. I would race to last-period class the next day to hear the rest of the story. "I want you to make connections between religion and your own lives," Sister said.

When she told the story of *Tommy*, for instance, she explained, "You know we live in a world of deceptive values that are imposed on us by other human beings, right? If we can smash through those illusions, maybe we can make our way back to God. We can get rid of society's blindness and the blindness we impose on ourselves. Because that's what you need to do. You need to work to overcome your own blindness."

"Wow," I thought. "This might make sense!"

Sister Donna Michelle's class pushed me to look at life through a different lens, and I finally felt like maybe I understood a little bit about religion for the first time. Funny that after nine years of Catholic school it took the Who to do it. When *Tommy* came out as a movie a year or two later, I was psyched. I went to see it at least five times. I bought the glossy movie book, and I knew every word of the soundtrack by heart.

Unfortunately—but perhaps predictably, given her open-minded outlook—Sister Donna Michelle left partway through the school year. She quit the sisterhood, married, and began working at a local pizzeria owned by her new husband. I missed her, but I was happy for her. I had already discovered pizza's spiritual power and its ability to solve problems.

Our substitute teacher was dreadful. She took us straight back to rote learning and memorization. I read books to get through the rest of my time in religion class. My friend Karen found that quite amusing. "You're reading *Gone with the Wind*?" she asked incredulously.

"Better than listening to this nonsense," I replied.

Karen and I talked about school and music. She was quiet, serious, and reserved. I was loud, outspoken, and opinionated. As our friendship rekindled during junior year, we became inseparable. Karen was desperate to see live music, too. We took the high-speed line to the Tower and saw Peter Frampton, the Tubes, Robert Palmer, and Lou Reed. We told my parents we were going with a group of friends, and they acquiesced. I think they realized how important music was to me—at least my mother did. She wanted me to be happy.

My father was more concerned with keeping me safe, and he was not totally wrong in his hunch that concerts unleashed a wildness in kids that could be risky. At least once I found myself in need of protection—when Queen came to the Civic Center. The concert was general admission, no assigned seating. I was, of course, determined to get right up front. My friends and I arrived early and ended up smashed against the glass entrance doors before security opened them. When the guards finally pushed open the doors, I was propelled backward while my friends were pushed forward into the venue. Another glass door opened behind me, sandwiching me between the two doors. This was two years before the fatal concert crush that took the lives of eleven fans at a Who concert in Cincinnati, so no one was yet considering the potential for disaster.

As more and more people streamed inside the concert hall, the heavy entrance doors on either side of me squeezed me tighter. The force pressed all the air out of my lungs; I couldn't even take a breath. I knew I was going to pass out and die if I didn't do something. I felt intense fear and panic. With all the strength I could summon, I pushed the door forward with Herculean effort and extricated myself. The experience was terrifying—like being buried in a coffin—and this incident likely contributed to my horrible claustrophobia later in life. Of course, my immediate priority was still to get up in front of the stage and hopefully rejoin my friends.

The Civic Center staff tried clumsily to control the flow of the crowd. Two security guards used a long piece of lumber about eight feet long as a barricade. They would lift up the plank to let a few people at a time onto the floor; then they would slam the board back down. While the board was up, I darted forward, but they brought the board down hard and smashed my hand. My left index finger was definitely broken, but I still pressed ahead to the front. The throbbing pain in my hand was momentarily secondary to the majesty of Freddie Mercury—prancing along the front of the stage with his signature broken microphone stand, commanding the audience—and the powerful artistry of John Deacon, Brian May, and Roger Taylor.

The next day at school my finger and hand were black and blue and grotesquely swollen. I was in excruciating pain, but I had to wait until the end of the school day to go to the hospital. I told my dad I had hurt my hand doing gymnastics in PE class at school. Any other explanation would certainly have meant no more concerts.

Soon I was attending about three concerts a month. I devoured all the rock-and-roll fan magazines—*Circus*, *Hit Parader*, and *Creem*—to soak up information on my favorite bands and to discover new ones.

My sister got to see David Bowie at the Tower Theater on his Diamond Dogs tour—a show that was recorded for his *David Live* album. I first saw Bowie live when he returned to Philly during his Isolar–1976 tour in support of *Station to Station*. I begged my friend Rosemary to join me. "You will *love* Bowie," I told her. "Even if you're not a fan now, I promise you that you will be."

The show started with strange images projected onto a screen, and then lots of bright white lights against a simple black backdrop. David wore a white shirt and black vest; he was captivating in all his beauty. As we drove home in her silver Camaro, Rosemary said: "Oh my God, you're right. I am definitely a Bowie fan now." I was graduating from fan to rock-and-roll recruiter.

During this time, I began working at McDonald's. I worked from 4 p.m. to 1 a.m. to save money to buy concert tickets and cool outfits. I also needed plenty of Love's Fresh Lemon cologne and Lemon Up shampoo. I brought leftover Big Macs and Quarter Pounders with cheese home to my father, and he took them to work for his lunch, which helped when I wanted to go to concerts. I was like a burglar bringing a fat, juicy steak to a guard dog—except I was looking to break out of the house, not into it.

A weekend without a show was miserable. Concerts were mind-expanding: beautiful people hanging in the aisles, drunks fighting, couples making out, people spaced out on a variety of drugs from Quaaludes to LSD. I found it exhilarating to meet new people and flirt with cute guys who looked nothing like the boys in my high school. The camaraderie of shows and the social atmosphere of the crowd kept me going. Being with other kids my own age who enjoyed the same music made me feel a part of something much bigger. My Catholic schoolgirl horizons were expanding at a rapid pace.

Not everyone felt the same way about my music obsession. My friends from elementary school and most of the kids in my high school thought I was weird or on drugs. So I gravitated toward a small group of people who felt the same way about music and the world that I did, and we formed a tight bond that left me impervious to attack.

Camping out for tickets was often as much fun as going to a concert itself. Of course, these were the days before massive ticket-sales companies and corporations bought out the front rows of concert venues. In the '70s, you were pretty much guaranteed seats in the first three rows in the pit at the Tower Theater or Spectrum if you got in line early enough. Karen and our friends Pete, Joe, Greg, and I would take the first early morning train out of Norristown to Philadelphia and then walk the twelve or so blocks to Eighteenth and Lombard, where the Electric Factory office was located. It was an urban adventure. Some mornings it was freezing cold, and I'd be bundled up in my brown suede wrap coat with its huge fur collar.

I met so many cool, interesting, and eccentric people in those lines: photographers, artists, musicians, models, and a few high school kids from other suburban towns. I met Patti Brett there. She was one of the "Sigma Kids"—a small group of die-hard Bowie fans who kept a nightly vigil outside of Sigma Sound Studios at Twelfth and Race Streets in Philly in 1974 when Bowie was recording his groundbreaking *Young Americans* album. One night during that vigil, Bowie invited Patti and a handful of Sigma Kids into the studio to hear the record and give their feedback. She had her photo taken with him. I was so envious. Patti was a *legend* to me. At the beginning of "All the Young Dudes" on the *Live* album, after Bowie sings, "Billy rapped all night 'bout his suicide," you can clearly hear someone say

"Pat!" I always thought it was Bowie, speaking to Patti.

Years later, I found out the real story from Patti: "Around the thirty-second mark," she told me, "you can hear Joey McDevitt yell out my name. He was in the second row, orchestra pit, and I was seated in front of him. He kept trying to push his chair into the front row, and it was annoying me. I told him if he did it again, I was going to hit him. Sure enough, he did it again, and I hit him, and he yelled out my name. He was being a pain, but I couldn't ask for a better gift!"

While camping out, I also met Charlie Carroll, who looked just like Cheetah Chrome from the Dead Boys, and two artists named Peter and Chuck, who were so beyond cool that I couldn't even speak to them, even after they invited us back to their apartment one day. Peter and Chuck were brilliant and worldly and bitingly sarcastic and funny. Their hair was dyed like rock stars', and their clothing mirrored that of their idols. One whole wall of Peter and Chuck's apartment was filled with crucifixes of varying styles and designs. Near the bathroom was a giant wooden portrait of Chuck with a little door on his pants that opened. To me, the other guests in the apartment seemed to be models, poets, rock stars, and other rising superstars. Just being in Chuck and Peter's presence made me feel cool by association.

The atmosphere in line for tickets was always joyful and convivial. On our way back to the train, we'd stop at H. A. Winston's for onion soup and strawberry daiquiris. Liquor laws were much more relaxed back then. I felt chic and cosmopolitan on those outings—far removed from the suburban parochial schoolgirl I actually was.

In June 1976, the summer before my senior year, Karen and our friend Sharon from high school and I joined 105,000 other fans for an insane afternoon at JFK Stadium in South Philly, seeing Gary Wright, Peter Frampton, and Yes. I felt bad for the Pousette-Dart Band, who opened the show. They never stood a chance against a crowd waiting to see the main acts. Even the Philadelphia Mummers were booed off the stage. I'm not sure who thought it was a good idea to put a carnival-style parade troupe like the mummers on the bill at a rock concert. This was Philadelphia, after all—the city whose denizens threw snowballs at Santa Claus during an Eagles football game.

I had seen Frampton and Wright together a few months earlier at the Tower Theater, and I was torn about sharing them with such a huge audience. Gary Wright wouldn't normally have been an artist I'd have liked—there were almost no guitars on his album; his hit "Dream Weaver" was all synthesizer and keyboards. But that surreal, poetic record was a necessary soundtrack for my teenage escape, and certainly the perfect backdrop for a weed and drug-saturated crowd at JFK Stadium on a blazing hot day in 1976.

Like many sixteen-year-olds at the time, I adored Peter Frampton. That day, he basically re-created his *Frampton Comes Alive*, which was fine with me—I loved those songs. Peter always seemed as one with his guitar, as though it was a part of him. I found that fascinating. In between acts was a huge garbage toss, and people threw trash and fireworks everywhere for almost ten minutes straight.

Yes seemed to take forever to set up their equipment. By the time they were ready, somehow the weather had turned dark and cold. I only knew Yes's hit "Roundabout," and maybe one other tune. I wasn't into what I later learned was called prog rock. As a full moon rose over the stadium, the band took the stage draped in flowing white robes, and I was ready to go home. Being in a huge venue with so many people listening to music as the sun set around us was a truly moving experience, but I already preferred smaller, more intimate engagements.

❧

By the end of high school, my musical tastes had grown edgier. My older, male, gay high school friends—Pete, Greg, and Joe—introduced me to music by the New York Dolls, Iggy Pop, the Ramones, Patti Smith, the Runaways, and Blondie. These female-fronted bands, especially, intrigued me. I couldn't play an instrument, and I most definitely could not sing, but I was empowered by the strength of these women, as well as their talent, style, and guts. I started to dress the way I wanted, with lots of satin, lace, suede, and leather, and I definitely spoke up more often. I disagreed with my teachers on politics and literature, but I felt better able to support my point of view. I began fighting for gender equality in my Catholic school and my fast-food job. And I called people out on their bullshit.

My school was predominantly white, and I didn't have much interaction with people of color until working at McDonald's where I met Tyrell, who was Black. I loved Tyrell, and I enjoyed working shifts with him. He had a great sense of humor and enjoyed a good prank or a food fight. One day before work, my coworkers and I were sitting in a booth drinking sodas and eating cheeseburgers. These friends, some whom I knew from high school, started to make racist jokes, some about Tyrell, who was not present. I knew that if I said something, these kids would probably not be my friends anymore, but I had to do something. My speaking out that day definitely marked a transition from childhood to adulthood. My friends never did speak to me again, but I knew I'd done the right thing. I didn't tell Tyrell or anyone else what had happened, but when confronted with racism for the first time in my life, I knew where I stood.

Though people often let me down, music never did. As I listened to more music and developed as an individual, I wanted to be a person who sought out her own music rather than had it dictated to her by a radio station. I started understanding that I was angry and discontented, a marginalized nonconformist who felt stifled at home and school. I searched for music that fed my restless, dissatisfied feelings. Loud, angry, and adventurous music empowered me. It introduced me to a new world that was wider and vastly different from the one where I lived—a place from which I desperately wanted to escape.

Patti Smith soon became one of my first female role models. She was as tough and badass as the boys, but she also read poetry and literature. If she

PATTY SMITH

Patti Smith is definitely one of the greatest performers of this decade. She and her band have the ability to drive audiences into a frenzy. Friday night, December 17, was no exception.

The evening began with a first class performance by Sparks, with those adorable Mael brothers, Russell and Ron. It was hard to decide who was the star of the show—Russell who pranced and danced all over the stage, or Ron, who sat stone-faced at the keyboards. Sparks' music has taken a change for the better. They have dropped the simpler, high voiced melodies and have turned into a hard rock band.

Patti's show started with **We're Going to Have a Real Good Time Tonight**. And she was right. Dressed in gold satin gym short, a ripped T-shirt and high topped sneakers with their laces wound around her ankles, she looked more like an orphan than a budding rock-star.

Her performance was terrific, as she danced, sang, teased and taunted from the moment she stepped onto the stage until the end. Patti seemed to use the audience as a prop, when she jumped into the crowd, and let one lucky boy sing with her. Her best numbers that evening were **Gloria, Free Money, Ask the Angels, Ain't It Strange,** and **Pumpin.** After the encore, **My Generation** she had the audience on their feet, screaming and begging for more. When the night had ended the exhausted audience left Tower, thoroughly drained of all energy but ready to go back as soon as Patti Smith returns to Philly again.

Nancy Petriello 8A

Letting my Catholic high school peers know about Sparks and Patti Smith— even if the school paper typesetter spelled her name wrong in the headline.

referred to a poet or author like Rimbaud or William Burroughs, I ran out and read their works immediately. I bought a men's white button-down shirt and a skinny black tie to re-create Patti's look from the cover of her *Horses* album. When the movie *Annie Hall* came out, the menswear look took off, but I knew who'd really started that trend.

We camped out for Patti Smith tickets and got front-row seats. I remember walking down the aisle of the Tower Theater with Pete the night of the show, when he noticed two older folks sitting in the eleventh row. "I bet they're Patti's parents," he whispered.

"No way, really?" I said.

"Let's go talk to them!" He walked right down their row and said, "Hi, are you Patti Smith's parents?"

"Why yes, we are," replied Patti's mother, Beverly.

"We *love* your daughter," Pete and I gushed.

I asked Patti's mom if I could write her a letter. I don't know what made me ask that, but she obligingly scribbled her address in New Jersey down on a piece of paper. I corresponded with Beverly Smith for years after meeting her. She sent me autographed pictures of her daughter and guitarist Lenny

I loved the way Nils Lofgren played guitar, and I had the biggest crush on him when I was sixteen.

VIEW

Nils Lofgren—"Night after Night"
by Nancy Petriello

Nils Lofgren has been around for quite a while. You might remember him as Neil Young's lead guitarist and piano player. He was also a member of the band "Crazy Horse" and had his own group "Grin." Critics have praised Nils as being America's best native guitarist and many thought him to be the most appropriate replacement for Mick Taylor of the Rolling Stones. As one critic put it, "You couldn't assemble a better Rolling Stone if they came in do-it-yourself kits." Yet Nils Lofgren still remains generally unknown.

But not for long—because Nils has just put out a sensational live album which will surely sweep him to stardom. There are few artists who write, sing, and play all their own songs and then are able to perform them as perfectly and with such vitality as Lofgren. And few live albums contain the energy found in this one.

Nils rips through tunes like "Back It Up," "Keith Don't Go" and "Beggars Day" with such a passion it could melt your turntable. When he's not raging through fiery guitar solos he's tearing away at the piano. The best cut on the album is definitely Nils self proclamation, "I Came to Dance", which in it's autobiographical style, says it all. "Night after Night" is truly one of the finest live albums ever made. But don't take my word for it. Buy it —and treat yourself to some pure, unadulterated Rock and Roll.

Kaye, and told me little stories about Patti growing up. She would report where in the world Patti was on tour. She asked about my life in high school. Those letters are so precious to me.

That night at the Tower Theater, I gave Patti roses, which she proceeded to eat onstage in front of me.

A few months later, I also sat in the front row for Iggy Pop. In the middle of his set, I felt compelled to run up to the stage. When I reached him, Iggy grabbed me and planted a big, sloppy (and welcome) kiss on me. I was sixteen, and the effect was powerful. For months, people came up to me and said, "Hey, you're that girl Iggy Pop kissed!" I wore that title like a badge of honor.

Months later, I sat in the front row for Cheap Trick. I dashed up to the stage again, this time securing a much more polite smooch from Robin Zander.

I loved the way Nils Lofgren played guitar, and I stalked him when he performed at Montgomery County Community College, a few miles from my home. I made a scrapbook for him and showed it to a photographer before the show, who told Nils about it. I nearly melted when the photographer found me and said, "Nils wants to meet you." The photos from that day epitomize all that is the '70s, from my silk kimono and granny glasses to Nils's vest and gold chain.

After Gerry joined the army and I started going to more shows, I wasn't really interested in high school boys. I dated a lifeguard and a guy I met at McDonald's, but I was mostly focusing on experiencing music. That October 1976, I was seventeen, and I snuck up to New York City to see the premiere of Led Zeppelin's movie *The Song Remains the Same* with my older friend Dale, whom I met camping out for tickets. I wasn't sure if it was a "date" or not, but I liked the idea of the adventure. The premiere was on a Wednesday, very much a "school night," but in the days before cell phones and electronic leashes, I figured I could pull it off.

Arriving in New York, we encountered a street protest related to the upcoming presidential election. People were chanting: "Ford and Carter are both the same!" People weren't happy with the two-party system even then. I was intrigued by the majesty and grandeur around me, and the hustlers, prostitutes, and freaks we saw in Times Square. New York was sinister and menacing, but it was also thrilling and invigorating.

Dale and I dashed through the crowds to reach the cinema. We hoped to catch a glimpse of the band members, who were supposed to be in attendance—but we had a hard time because *everyone* there looked like a rock star. The movie itself was long but hypnotic. Especially for the premiere, the theater installed a quadraphonic sound system, so the experience was exhilarating and a little trippy. I found the fantasy scenes weird and a bit self-indulgent, but I was a seventeen-year-old from the suburbs, so what did I know?

Somehow, I made it back home just before my 12:30 a.m. curfew, but it only took my mom five minutes to figure out what I had done. I let something slip about tolls—and there were no tolls on the road to Philly, where she thought I had gone.

"You went to New York City?" she exclaimed, appalled at my nerve.

"Who do you think you are?" She set my punishment nine months in advance: "You're grounded. Come June, they'll be no senior week for you." And she kept her word. Not that it bothered me much. I didn't care about going down the Jersey Shore for senior week with a bunch of drunken jocks and rah-rahs anyway. At least she didn't tell my father, as the penalty would have been much worse.

Meanwhile, I was lucky that my mother still allowed me to go to concerts around Philly.

At that first Iggy Pop show—featuring David Bowie on keyboards, no less—the opening act was Blondie. I became obsessed with Debbie Harry. I wanted to be Debbie Harry. I cut and dyed my hair like hers, and I copied her outfits from album covers and magazines. I thought she was the most beautiful and talented woman in the world. I knew nothing about *playing* music, but I appreciated talent.

In comparison to my gay friends Pete, Greg, and Joe, everyone else at my school seemed like philistines. Those guys were only a year or two older than me, but they were intellectual, sarcastic, well-read, and cultured. They debated movies, art, literature, and politics, and they knew where everything was happening in the city. Notably, one of the things they knew best was how to have fun. I sat back and absorbed it all—finally a willing student again. The trio further introduced me to Philadelphia's nightlife and club scene beyond the music world. After one concert, they snuck me into my first bar, a gay club called the Steps, where we sipped "iced teas" and danced to Donna Summer and Diana Ross late into the morning hours. I probably told my parents I was sleeping at a friend's house to get away with that one.

I was still in high school, but my world was expanding, and I was recognizing how important music, art, and culture were to who I was. I was ravenously hungry to learn more, and the late '70s offered plenty to feed that desire. There was always a concert, an event, or an experience waiting to broaden my mind and introduce me to new ideas. I was meeting people

I subscribed to Interview *magazine, and it felt like I stalked Andy Warhol around New York and Pennsylvania. He was always really cool to me. This shot with Karen is from Philadelphia, 1979.*

who were brilliant, charming, and interesting and who wanted to make their mark on the world. I couldn't wait to get my own apartment in the city so I could wake up and be part of it all.

I started following Andy Warhol's career and projects, and I began reading *Interview* magazine. I liked how Andy saw the world. When I heard he was coming to a bookstore in Philadelphia, Karen and I went to meet him, and I got my books signed and my photo taken with him. Later I stalked him at the One Fifth bar on Fifth Avenue, and then in a parking lot in New York City. He was always incredibly nice.

The photographer I'd met at the Nils Lofgren show called me one day and told me the Ramones were playing at the University of Pennsylvania. My sister had just gotten her license, and I persuaded her to drive us. We arrived at Houston Hall just in time to see the Ramones take the stage. There was something special about that band—they embodied an entirely new genre of music, a backlash against progressive rock and even some of the bands I loved, like Led Zeppelin. The Ramones' music was raw and lyrically simplistic, but the immediacy had its own heartbeat—one I felt merging with my own.

❦

I had always enjoyed learning—or tried—but now high school left me uninterested, bored, and resentful. My high school teachers were uninspiring. I got in trouble for the most ridiculous things in high school—like eating an apple in an assembly, or wearing photochromic transition lenses, which had just been invented. The lenses darkened and became sunglasses outdoors, and didn't transition back to regular eyeglasses very quickly in those days. My school actually let kids go outside to smoke. I did not have that habit, but my friends did, and I enjoyed being outside, so I would join them. When the bell rang, I would scurry back into the building with the lenses still dark, and the nuns would scream, "Take those sunglasses off!" I needed my glasses to see; I had to stumble and find my way to my seat half blind.

During my senior year, I took Business English, held in the same room as a class named Great Books. Each week I "borrowed" a new book, classics like *Silas Marner*, *Madame Bovary*, and *Tess of the D'Urbervilles*. Reading was still one of my favorite hobbies. Regrettably, *Catcher in the Rye* went back on the shelf—I thought it was about farming. I probably would have viewed Holden Caulfield as a kindred spirit, because I hated phonies just as much as he did.

My mind wasn't idle. During my classes, I sat in the back and imagined how I could make the same lesson more interesting and fun if I were a teacher. I daydreamed about connecting students to their learning, so the experience didn't seem so dry and boring. For one thing, I would incorporate issues and topics teenagers cared about. I wouldn't humiliate my students; I would treat them with respect and love.

If diminutive tormentor Sister Alice and the other teachers at Bishop Kenrick were my role models, I knew that I would be an *anti-teacher*: I would do the complete opposite of what these people had done to me. I confess that I still owe a great debt of gratitude to my instructors at Bishop Kenrick High School, mainly because they showed me how *not* to treat kids.

Fortunately, my high school graduation was looming, but I was still unsure of what career to pursue. My dad shut down the idea of teaching, and there was no arguing with him: "You'll be a glorified babysitter. And kids today are dangerous. You'll get hurt." My dad had heard horror stories about the local public high school, and had seen movies like *Blackboard Jungle* and *To Sir, With Love*.

Lingering over some career advisory books in the school library, I read about the paralegal profession, still a relatively new field. If I couldn't be a teacher or a Shaolin monk, I figured this might be an interesting job. I mentioned my discovery to my dad. "Why don't you be a lawyer?" he replied.

"How about I start off as a paralegal?" I countered. "If I like it, I'll become a lawyer." I thought being a paralegal might be fun. I liked reading and writing; maybe I would be good at it. I found a school two hours away that offered a legal-assistant major. Soon it was arranged; in the fall, I would go off to Harrisburg, Pennsylvania, to Central Pennsylvania Business School to earn an associate's degree.

I graduated in 1977, and I looked forward to moving away from my childhood home and launching a new life. I was anxious to put nuns, priests, draconian rules, and high school politics behind me. The world outside the stifling Catholic school microcosm seemed boundless. I wouldn't miss school uniforms, endless judgment, or dull lessons, and I welcomed college-level learning and stimulating grown-up experiences. I knew I'd still keep in touch with my little nucleus of high school friends, but I was ready to sail into uncharted territory.

With my college boyfriend Steve and my friend Audrey, before heading to the Class 1 disco.

4
WORKING HARD IN HARRISBURG

ARRISBURG, THE CAPITAL CITY OF PENNSYLVANIA, was a strange, surreal place compared to Philly. There was not much to do at school, or anywhere else in the city. I decided to room with a girl I knew from elementary and high school named Denise Milus, whom I called Dee. We weren't close friends, but we liked each other well enough. We both figured that rooming together would eliminate the chance of experiencing some of the horror stories we had heard—even though Dee came into the dorm expecting the worst.

"I thought you were on drugs back then," she told me later. "I was relieved to discover during our first week as roommates that you weren't." On the contrary, Dee also wanted to be a paralegal, and we became study partners.

Within the first week at Central Penn, Dee and I learned that if we wanted to have fun, we would have to make our own entertainment. We were two young women on our own for the first time at the height of the disco era. Even though I had consumed every page of *Punk* magazine and owned nearly every album covered in its pages, I'm not going to lie—I enjoyed some disco, and I loved to dance. As long as I could be connected to music in some way, I was happy.

College life wasn't quite the stirring experience I had hoped for. The students at Central Penn were mostly women from the surrounding area.

They were nice but a bit conservative and dull. I realized quickly how lucky I was to room with Dee, who was always ready to have fun, even if that only meant walking down to the local McDonald's and goofing on the local boys we met there. If any bands were playing in clubs in Harrisburg, I didn't know where to find them. So Dee and I threw parties in our dorm room, fueled with Riunite wine and punk and disco music.

After a few months, I met a friend named David who worked at the local McDonald's. He was gay and reminded me of my gay friends from home, whom I missed terribly. David liked music and art and nightlife. He could be scathing and witty, which was always a prerequisite for any of my friends. We clicked instantly. David introduced me to a whole new world of gay and transgender discophiles in Harrisburg.

With no live music in the city, I frequented discos nearly every Thursday, Friday, and Saturday night during my two years at Central Penn. Disco music was anathema to punk, but I didn't police myself. If I liked a song, and it made me feel something, I didn't care what genre it was. I had plenty of Sylvester, Gloria Gaynor, Evelyn "Champagne" King, and Cheryl Lynn records in my collection. I even choreographed a dance routine based around the hustle, and Dee and I won several local dance contests. One night out at Class 1, the local disco, I met a heart-stoppingly beautiful young man named Steve, who swept me off my feet. Steve liked disco and punk, too. He was an incredible dancer, a sharp dresser, and a sweet, kind person. Steve had been raised by his grandparents, and some weekends we'd escape the disco scene and drive to Steve's home an hour away in Mifflintown, Pennsylvania, where we'd watch TV and eat pickles and pretzels with his grandma and grandpa.

Despite some wonderful times together, I suspected Steve might be gay. We broke up after about six months of dating, when he came out. We stayed friends into the 1980s, but sadly, Steve contracted AIDS while in the Air Force, and he died in 1989.

I danced to disco while still listening to Queen, Aerosmith, and Led

Zeppelin, yet my central focus and true loves slowly became new wave and punk. Besides adoring Patti Smith, Blondie, and Iggy, I worshipped the Ramones, Eddie and the Hot Rods, the Sex Pistols, the Damned, the Buzzcocks, the Cramps, the Dead Boys, the Pretenders, Elvis Costello, Generation X, and, especially, the Clash. I craved the energy—the music fed the rebellious feelings inside of me and inspired and sustained my objections to conformity. Simply put, the sound of punk was a cry for change.

I appreciated punk's anti-fashion stance and the toughness of its aesthetic: leather jackets and boots, vintage dresses and skirts, homemade T-shirts. I felt protected when dressed as a punk. I took my white Patti Smith button-down shirt and splattered it with red paint and Clash lyrics. Punk clothing sent a clear message to people: "Don't fuck with me." That was a message I often felt I needed to deliver as a young woman in the late 1970s.

Unfortunately, no one at my college shared my love of punk, or was even aware of half the bands that I adored so completely. I was devastated when I heard Marc Bolan was killed in a car accident in September 1977. I took to my bed weeping—but no one else at my school had ever heard of T. Rex, except for being vaguely aware of their hit "Bang a Gong (Get it On)." A month later, the college practically shut down when three members of Lynyrd Skynyrd were killed in a plane crash.

I needed a connection to the outside punk-loving world, so I found a pen pal from New Orleans in the classified ads in *Punk* magazine. His name was "Silver Adams," real name Cyril, and he told me about a punk rock band from near him called the Normals.

When I was home on school break, Karen and I went to Philly to see the Normals play. They were awesome, and they hung out with us afterward and talked. I dug their Southern accents. I liked being around musicians and seeing behind the curtain of how bands functioned on both practical and musical levels. That show was my first visit to the Hot Club, Philly's premier punk club, and I enjoyed it so much that I knew I'd be back. The Hot Club was different than a concert hall or disco—it was personal, intimate, and freeing. The crowd was entirely nonjudgmental, and the rock stars onstage were completely accessible. Being right up against the stage and close to the band was so much better than sitting in a seat in the audience.

Meanwhile, studying to be a paralegal didn't bring quite the intellectual stimulation I had hoped. I took classes in torts, corporate law, real estate law, and accounting. There were no Socratic seminars like I had seen in movies about college. My teachers were efficient, but a bit drab and colorless. I worked hard to earn good grades—I didn't dare bring home anything lower than a B—but the material did not excite me about a career in a law firm. I missed my family, and I called my mother often, even though she would scold me for running up the phone bill. I missed our talks and her friendship, and I counted the days before going home for school holidays.

Central Penn required that students attend a summer session, and fortunately the campus had a swimming pool. After class, I would work on my tan there. During the summer I met Debbie, a hairdresser at a neighborhood salon. She and I often drove around "the circuit" in downtown Harrisburg in her Mustang, like something out of the movie *American Graffiti*. We would end up at Denny's at four in the morning, eating French dip sandwiches and wishing for something more thrilling to come along.

During my second year of college, I made more friends off campus. One night Dee and I decided to have a party in our dorm suite. We invited some of my gay friends and some local guys who worked at a pizzeria, not really anticipating the issues that might arise. After quietly drinking in his chair for several hours, one of the pizzeria guys named Mike got up and punched my gay friend Gary in the mouth, knocking out his teeth and breaking his jaw. I jumped on Mike's back and threw him out the door, while my other friends rushed Gary to the hospital. I was terrified that I would be kicked out of school, but somehow we managed to keep the incident from college authorities. I had to testify in court a few months later, however, and Mike was ordered to pay restitution for the unprovoked attack.

❦

In March 1979, I discovered Roxy Music would be returning to the Tower Theater in Upper Darby, back in Philadelphia. Roxy Music's *Siren* was the first album I had ever bought with my own money, so the band was very special to me. I called my friend Frank, a Harrisburg local I'd met at a disco, as I knew he liked Roxy Music. "We have to be there, don't you think?"

"Definitely," Frank agreed. "Let's do it."

Despite the fact that I'd been living on my own at college for two years, my mother and father still had a firm grip on me. I was afraid of angering my father in anything I did, or at least anything he'd find out about. No way in hell would my parents have ever allowed me to leave school and take the two-hour train ride back to Philly. My dad's psychological hold on me remained firm. But I was young, bold, and feeling independent, and I figured my parents didn't need to know about my plan. I would go down for the show and come back the same night. I arranged to meet my high school friend Karen at the Tower.

My anticipation grew and grew over seeing Roxy Music for the second time. Meanwhile a strange and disconcerting event took place the Wednesday before the show. Unknown to me, my school was located a few miles away from a nuclear reactor, and that plant had experienced some sort of "accident." My roommate Dee and I watched the TV news coverage. I said, "Hey, this doesn't sound good to me. Something's not right here. This seems kind of *dangerous*."

But no one at my school seemed to take the incident too seriously. Barely anyone was even talking about Three Mile Island. So that Friday night, I jumped on the train with Frank and headed to see Roxy Music in Philly. On the way there, we passed within yards of the monstrous nuclear reactors, blinking in the dark. I had no idea of the gravity of the situation at the time. I just wanted to catch up with my friends and see one of my longtime favorite bands.

Two hours later, I arrived at the Tower Theater, and I felt the familiar pre-concert excitement. I found Karen right away. I hadn't seen her since Christmas, but instead of throwing her arms around me and greeting me with a smile, she was freaking out. Her hands were shaking. "Oh my God," she cried. "You *have* to call your mom!"

The truth about Three Mile Island had come out, and my parents were in full-blown panic. My mother had tried to get in touch with me at school, but she was unable to reach me. Thinking with her sixth sense, she figured my best friend would know where I was, and she tracked down Karen and begged: "If you know where Nancy is, please tell me." Karen had no choice; she had to let my mother know I was okay, and that I would even be in Philly that night.

I dashed to a pay phone to call my house. I prayed my dad wouldn't answer the phone—but of course he did. My hands shook as I gripped the receiver. I knew I was in enormous, gigantic trouble. Instead, my father was so relieved I was no longer in Harrisburg that he didn't yell or scream. "Where are you?" he asked.

"I'm at a concert at the Tower Theater in Upper Darby."

"Take the train to Norristown after the show and get home," he ordered.

But now I was worried about my friend Frank. He wasn't a boyfriend, but I didn't want to send him back alone to what we now knew was a nuclear meltdown.

"I have a friend with me, dad. If things are bad in Harrisburg, do you think he should go back?"

"Okay, just bring him home with you," my dad said. This was one of two times my father was tremendously cool to me when I needed him the most.

While Frank and I spent the weekend in Norristown, I obsessed over tests and papers due in school the following week. Late on Sunday, against my parents' better judgment, I headed back to Central Penn, only to find out our school was closed for a week due to the unprecedented and historical nuclear emergency. In typical college student fashion, we used the opportunity to throw a weeklong "Nuclear Meltdown" party, a welcome respite after a challenging year of reading legal briefs and studying contracts. We laughed as we reenacted *Saturday Night Live*'s hysterical "Pepsi Syndrome" skit.

When I felt anxiety or terror creep over me about the situation, I stifled it. The news was filled with dire warnings, so we turned it off. If someone was freaking out, we handed them a beer. Most of my classmates had returned to their homes in the local area, so Dee and I and the handful of students remaining blasted my punk records and danced in the hallways. We felt certain that everything had to be under control, so why not take advantage of the break? When school didn't reopen after a week, my father sent my little brother Danny with his brand-new driver's license up to Central Penn to bring Dee and me home. We stayed home another week before school resumed.

Though I danced through the thick of it, not until years later did I learn how serious the situation at Three Mile Island had been. The partial meltdown was the worst nuclear disaster in US history. The incident resulted in two million people being exposed to supposedly small amounts of dangerous radioactive gases. I will never forget the fear, confusion, and end-of-the-world panic of that weekend despite the fact that my youth prevented me from truly believing I'd experience any real harm.

When I graduated from Central Penn in the summer of 1979, I thought about staying in the Harrisburg area. Dee secured a job at the statehouse, and she had fallen in love with a guy from the area. She was staying. I had grown to love the little city, and I'd made some great friends outside of school. I also enjoyed the freedom I had away from my strict parents. I was terrified to return to Norristown to begin living at home again.

My mother said, "Okay, I'll give you the summer to find a job there." I half-heartedly went on a few job interviews at local law firms, but I spent most of that time at parties and clubs or staying up all night with my friends. In a wild coincidence, one of the jobs I applied for was with the lawyer who represented Mike, the guy who attacked my friend the night of our party. I couldn't run out of that office fast enough. By August, my mom said, "I'm not financing your good times in Harrisburg," and she yanked me back to their house in Norristown.

5

PHILLY LOVE

BACK AT HOME AFTER GRADUATING with an associate's degree in a field I found boring and mind-numbing, I grew afraid that I would never find viable employment and make a real leap into adulthood. I searched for jobs, but I hated the phoniness of interviewing. I couldn't tell an employer where I saw myself in five years. I had trouble articulating my "growth trajectory." Honestly, I had a hard time mustering up excitement about being a paralegal at all. I didn't want to sit in a law library doing endless research. I wasn't interested in organizing files or writing up boilerplate documents. I also didn't feel I'd learned enough in college to be competent, and I didn't like to do anything if I wasn't good at it.

My mother was methodical and practical, and she took charge. "I got you a meeting at an employment agency in Norristown," she said. "You can type. They'll find you a job."

Mom was right. The owner quickly got me an interview at a huge law firm in the majestic Philadelphia Savings Fund Society Building in Philadelphia, right across the street from Reading Terminal Market. My mother and I took the train together for the interview in Center City. I was sweating through my blue business suit in the August heat.

My mom always made me feel relaxed and self-assured. "Of course you can be a paralegal," she said. "You're smart, and you work hard. What's the problem?"

Getting ready to hit the Hot Club. DENISE MILUS

During my interview, the human resources manager at Cohen, Shapiro, Polisher, Shiekman, and Cohen said, "Look, we have no paralegal positions available, but we are getting some new, state-of-the-art Wang computer equipment, and we're starting a word-processing department. Are you interested in being a word processor?"

I had no idea what a word processor was. Desperate for a job, of course I immediately said, "Oh yes, definitely!"

My mother and I ate club sandwiches at a little coffee shop across the street from the PSFS Building after the interview. I was a nervous wreck, but my mother said she was confident I had presented myself well. Sure enough, by the time our train pulled into Main Street–Norristown Station, I had a job offer. I was terrified but excited.

For the first few months, I commuted to Philly on the train. Because the firm's computer equipment wouldn't arrive for a few months, I worked as a "floater" wherever needed. In that role, I was able to quickly learn the tasks of every support staff position, from answering phones to making copies to typing up documents. I set up luncheons and delivered paperwork. I enjoyed doing something different every day, and I got to know most of the lawyers and staff in the multi-floored offices. I made friends quickly, going out for lunch with the other women, who shared office gossip and stories about their own lives.

Living at home as a twenty-year-old after being on my own at college for two years was extremely difficult. My dad imposed new rules and curfews. I had to be home by midnight, and I had to give him a detailed itinerary of where I was going and with whom. My brother Danny, my high school friend Karen, and I still went to concerts. After shows at the Tower Theater, we spent many late nights at Hannigans, the bar next door to the Tower Theater, drinking Miller High Life, "the champagne of beers." I snuck down to private parties there, like one where I met the Knack, the power pop masters of "My Sharona" fame. These nights were so much fun, but I paid for it when I got home with lots of screaming and yelling from my dad. I wanted my own place. Every day I checked the apartment listings in the *Philadelphia Inquirer.*

One day on my lunch break, I looked at a studio apartment at the Adelphia House on the corner of Thirteenth and Chestnut, less than half a block away from my job. The place was tiny: one room with a mini refrigerator and a two-burner stove, and a blue rug that looked like Astroturf. The bathroom barely contained a toilet, a sink, and a shower stall. The only window looked out at the fourteen-story warehouse of the John Wanamaker department store. Scrawled on the faded yellow wallpaper in the bathroom was one word: "Lonely." But the space was cozy, and I visualized how I would decorate it. The rent was $190 a month, exactly what I made in a week. I moved in on December 1, 1979.

Living in Center City Philadelphia was a little scary and dangerous. Crime was high, and stories of murders, rapes, and robberies filled the newspapers. I was a young woman on my own, living a Mary Tyler Moore adventure about which I had dreamed my whole life.

I loved the gritty and colorful cityscape that unfurled before me each morning. An old woman hawked socks on the corner, screeching, "*KNEE* highs, girls! *KNEE* highs!" Dreadlocked MOVE members sold T-shirts, incense, and necklaces in the shape of Africa on the corner of Twelfth and Chestnut. Three-card monte hustlers seemed to be everywhere. I frequently bought goods from the Asian purse sellers. The city was a wild, loud backdrop full of bright sights, sounds, and smells. I was elated to find myself in the middle of it.

Straightaway, I had trouble budgeting my money. I often spent too much on things I needed less than I needed food—like an eighty-dollar zebra-print sweater from Knit Wit. I often lived on burgers from Gino's, the fast-food restaurant across the street from the Adelphia House, or cans of Beefaroni from the 7-Eleven at Thirteenth and Walnut. The ubiquitous soft-pretzel sellers on every corner in the city always offered cheap sustenance.

At first, I was frightened to go out in Philly at night by myself. Then one day while I was walking down Chestnut Street, my college friend Bob appeared out of nowhere, grabbed me by the neck, and screamed, "Oh my God, Nancy Petriello!"

Back in Harrisburg, Bob and I would listen to records, put eye makeup on each other, and talk about punk bands. He was incredibly smart, sarcastic, and well-read. I hadn't seen Bob for over a year, but he lived only a few blocks away from me in Philly. Suddenly I had a partner in crime.

Though I was still slightly underage, I had a New Jersey license saying I was twenty-two—an ID someone had left the McDonald's where I worked in high school. In those days, New Jersey driver's licenses did not have photos. As long as you memorized your address and knew your zodiac sign and birth date, you would easily be cleared for entry to any bar or club.

Bob and I made a headquarters of the Hot Club, just a twenty-minute walk from our apartments, a place from which we could easily stumble home. The Hot Club was a tiny, sweaty place, and we *always* had fun there. The patrons were eclectic and interesting, and some had a dangerous edge. The stage at the Hot Club was only a few feet high, and it was easy to get right up front. After a spirited show—by the B-52's, for example—I would leave with a line of bruises along my thighs at the exact height of the stage. I felt like I was *in* the band when I saw a show at the Hot Club.

I was fascinated by Philly bands that played the Hot Club, like the Sic Kidz, the Proteens, and the Warm Jets, because I could just as easily see those people walking down the street as I could watch them onstage. The Sic Kidz had a female bass player named Alison, and I thought she was unbelievably cool. I got to know the musicians in the regular bands, and became fast friends with Tommy Ajax, the singer of the Proteens, and Mike Condi, their guitarist. The Proteens were still in high school, but they were playing in the hottest club in Philly. We'd drink together after shows or go for food at the Midtown Diner.

One of the greatest things about seeing bands at the Hot Club was that there were no boundaries between the performers and the audience. The setup was much different than seeing a band at the Spectrum, or even the Tower Theater. The local bands, especially, were so accessible. I started to form real friendships with many of them. Musicians would play onstage and then join us in the audience for the next band. Even when national acts came to town, the band members would hang out in the audience or smoke cigarettes outside the club, usually looking to strike up a conversation. I loved that intimacy. I also risked less chance of bouncers and security guards literally breaking my bones again like at the bigger shows I'd attended growing up.

Less than ten miles away in Cherry Hill, New Jersey, was the club Emerald City, formerly the Latin Casino, which in the 1960s and '70s had been home to performers like Harry Belafonte, Sammy Davis Jr., Lena Horne, and Dean Martin. I saw the Manhattan Transfer at the Latin Casino while I was in high school. But now Emerald City featured rock and new wave bands, and I saw the Ramones, the Romantics, the Buzzcocks, XTC, Gang of Four, the Pretenders, and the Psychedelic Furs there. The place was another rabbit hole to explore.

Once I went to see Squeeze over the New Jersey border at Emerald City with my friend Rosemary. As soon as we stepped out of the car, Rosemary realized she had locked her keys inside. "Oh no!" she screamed. "I need to get those keys! I gotta get back to Norristown or my parents will kill me!"

"Don't worry," I said. "We'll break in!"

Some guy smoking a cigarette in the parking lot saw our distress and came to our rescue. He somehow produced a coat hanger and helped us undo the latch and break into the car. "There you go!" he said. Once we heard his English accent, we realized Chris Difford from Squeeze had saved the day.

My friends Karen and Pete Bay got me tickets to see the Police in New Jersey. I had their *Outlandos d'Amour* album, and I really liked their brand of reggae punk. The venue was very untraditional, a roadhouse inn in the woods. And the opening band was the Cramps, about whom I knew nothing. When they took the stage, It was like getting bashed in the face. I couldn't tell if they were playing rockabilly, horror punk, surf music, or country/blues—but I was riveted. The most beautiful woman with a wild mane of hair was playing guitar—practically unheard of back then. That was Poison Ivy. Her husband, Lux Interior, was theatrical and iconic. I knew I was seeing something groundbreaking. Forget the Police—that night I became a huge Cramps fan. My gateway to punk was opening wider.

I loved to see female rockers, especially Joan Jett. She was a touring goddess who put her heart and soul into every performance. After a show, she was sweaty and spent, but she always ensured that her audience had a great time. I saw her once at Emerald City. I had just bought a pair of crazy black spandex pants, which I wore with super-high black stiletto heels and a green-and-black bumblebee-striped mohair sweater. I was coming out of the ladies' room when a very cute guy said to me: "Cool pants."

Life at the Fast Lane:
Joan Jett stage pass

"Thanks!" I said. We sat down together on the big couches in the lobby.

"Hi, I'm Eric," he said, and we started talking about the venue, music, and the Philadelphia area. We were in the middle of a great conversation when suddenly he jumped up and said, "Well, I have to go." I was crushed!

I thought he liked me, and I couldn't believe he was just going to blow me off. But as it turned out, Eric Ambel was the guitarist in Joan Jett's band, the Blackhearts, and he soon appeared onstage. That was a special show for me. Eric and I kept in touch, and he put me on the list for a bunch of Joan's shows, including a gig at the infamous Stone Pony in Asbury Park.

Eric visited me in Philly, and I took him to Third Street Jazz and Rock, the cool record store for "extreme music lovers," which featured the latest punk records as well as collectible vinyl. Eric turned me on to some new bands, including Motörhead. He showed me their album, and I thought they looked like a metal band. But then he got the guys at Third Street to play their song "Ace of Spades," on the store's sound system, and I was floored by their ferociousness.

Every day I was uncovering new opportunities to discover music and see live performances. I was meeting friends with the same interests and enjoying all that Philadelphia had to offer, which was plenty.

During the summer of 1980, I met the brilliant Lee Paris. He'd come to Philly from the University of California at Santa Cruz, where he had studied alternative media. He was now pursuing a master's degree in communication at the University of Pennsylvania. Lee and Steve Pross, aka Roid Kafka, had a radio show on WXPN called *Yesterday's Now Music Today*. Lee also promoted shows in Philly.

Preppy and prematurely balding, Lee was the unlikely "Philly scene leader" at the time, and I idolized him. He was funny and edgy and always at least five steps ahead of everyone else. Lee's sexuality was always a little bit ambiguous, but I wasn't interested in dating him. I just wanted to be in his world. Lee was an insomniac, and he'd often call me up in the middle of the night to chat. I loved listening to him talk about everything and everyone.

Lee, Frank Blank, and Denise Herman booked shows at Omni's, a new club at Ninth and Walnut, also a short distance from my house. Thanks to my fake ID, I was able to further feed my live-music craving. At Omni's, I saw bands and artists like Bunnydrums, Mission of Burma, Brian Brain, the Undead, the Fall, the Bush Tetras, and Nona Hendryx.

One night in September 1980, my friend Pete took me to New York to see David Bowie on stage in *The Elephant Man*. I wore a black jumpsuit with a big gold zipper down the front and black leather boots, and I felt like I was the height of sophistication and style. Before the show we visited Fiorucci, and I dreamed of someday owning something—*anything*—from that store. I had never been to the theater before, and I was surprised by how small it was and how close we were to Bowie. His brilliant, understated performance was riveting.

That same month, Lee Paris, Frank Blank, Ginny Traynor, her sister Lisa, and another visionary named David Wildman, working under the name Swingerz, rented out the Elks Center at Sixteenth and Fitzwater for a show with goth gods Bauhaus. When I walked into the dark, cavernous room with its huge, medieval windows and heard the eerie, pulsating boom of Bauhaus, I was overwhelmed. The band and the venue merged into a creepy, dark, visceral experience. The Elks Center was so mysterious and cool. I knew I wanted to come back to experience it again.

❦

My apartment decor could best be described as wall-to-wall "early Clash." When I moved to Philadelphia, I wanted leather pants so badly. I put this pair on layaway at the Knit Wit and visited them every week until I could afford to spring them from retail jail. I make no excuses for wearing them with white Nikes.
DENISE MILUS

By frequenting the Hot Club, Omni's, and other music venues, I met a crew of cool, smart, punk rock women who were totally connected to the scene: Sheva, Anne, Carol, and Lisa. They loved music as much as I did. They were all avid record collectors, and they knew the people at local radio stations and live music venues. Altogether, we always had an in to see and meet touring bands.

One day in mid-December 1980, Sheva told me: "We have to go see this band that's playing at the Bijou Café." Her friend at a radio station had told her that this band from Ireland was destined for greatness. That sounded enticing to me.

The forecast had predicted a blizzard for that evening, but since Sheva and I lived only a few blocks from the venue, we laced up our boots and trudged over. The band was called U2, and indeed they delivered as promised. They played that nearly empty room like they were playing a packed stadium. Afterward, we met and talked with the band members— who were stranded in Philly because of the storm. Honestly, they weren't punk enough for me. They seemed like nice enough guys, but I had difficulty understanding their thick Irish accents. I hounded my friends to leave.

A year later, on Saturday, May 30, 1981, I took my little brother, Danny, to New York City to see the Clash at Bond International Casino, a huge department store turned music venue in Times Square. The Clash were scheduled to play eight shows at Bond's to support their *Sandinista* album.

We got to the city early so we could shop and hang out on the Lower East Side. As I looked through the racks of clothing in a store called Trash and Vaudeville on St. Marks Place, Danny whispered to me: "Look, there's that singer guy from U2." I looked up and saw Bono saunter into the store. I hid behind the T-shirt display so he wouldn't see me and recognize me from the night of the blizzard. Later that afternoon, we saw John Belushi at another store on St. Marks Place. *Now* we were impressed!

My brother and I went to dinner at a little Italian restaurant in Soho. They had wine bottles lined all along the wall behind us. After we paid our bill, my brother looked at me with a mischievous grin. "I'm taking one of those bottles."

"Don't you dare!" I warned.

Before I could stop him, Danny grabbed a bottle and dashed out the door. We were laughing hysterically as we ran down the street. We didn't even notice the three men ahead of us until we crashed into them. Suddenly, right before us stood Mick Jones, Topper Headon, and Paul Simonon from the Clash. Our mouths dropped open. We froze in place. My brother handed the bottle of wine to Mick, hoping to get an autograph, but he was unable to articulate the request. "I—uh—can you—um—please," he stuttered. Mick smiled and said, "Thanks a lot, mate," and off they went with Danny's pilfered bottle of wine while we gasped and collapsed laughing on the sidewalk.

The Clash were the most important band to me back then. They were *everything*. Their music was passionate, angry, and political, but damn, they had great melodies, too. The Clash's experimentation with reggae, funk, and rock opened my ears to new styles of music. When I heard *London Calling* and, specifically, "Clampdown," with its reference to Harrisburg, I felt like Joe Strummer was speaking directly to *me*. I believed Joe was the sincerest rock artist around. He called out what was wrong in the world and then called upon kids to fight for change. I was definitely listening. I blared the Clash incessantly from my boom box as I walked the streets of Philadelphia, and Danny and I made homemade Clash T-shirts, many of which I still have today.

Sadly, the New York City Fire Department declared the event unsafe and canceled the band's performance that evening. They alleged—and the Clash later supported the claim—that greedy promoters had oversold the venue by double capacity. Outside Bond's, there was rioting in the streets as police on horseback beat back angry fans. We turned tail and retreated to Penn Station, dejected and crushed. For their part, the Clash made good on every ticket. Instead of eight shows, they performed a total of seventeen times in New York with incredible opening acts including Grandmaster Flash and the Furious Five, Bad Brains, Sugar Hill Gang, Dead Kennedys, Kraut, and the Fall. For my part, I never had enough money to return to New York City, so I missed out.

❧

On steamy summer nights in Center City Philadelphia, Lisa, Carol, and the rest of us sat on Anne and Sheva's apartment steps. They lived on the 1200 block of Spruce Street, a half block from where the shooting involving Mumia Abu-Jamal and police officer Daniel Faulkner took place. We escaped the heat and blasted the Clash from my boom box. "Get the hell out of here!" the prostitutes screamed as we invaded their workplace.

The blocks surrounding Thirteenth Street from Chestnut to Spruce were much different back then. The area was filthy, dangerous, and a bit threatening, especially at night. This was the meeting place for an assortment of grifters, street people, drug addicts, prostitutes, and criminals. We often saw fights and drug deals, but we didn't care. The rough setting was the perfect backdrop for our punk music.

My friends and I spent hours at the Midtown Diner after shows, eating thick cheeseburgers while we discussed each band's performance. Sheva, Carol, Anne, and Lisa always had the inside scoop on the musicians I loved, and our gossip sessions were lengthy. The Midtown never cared how long we stayed. Sometimes we were there until the wee hours of dawn as a revolving crew of punks joined us.

Besides going to shows, we frequented the many pinball machine arcades that lined Chestnut Street. We played the pinball tables, especially *Flash Gordon* and *Medusa*, air hockey, and the brand-new *Space Invaders* video games, or we went to one of Philly's many movie theaters to watch *Apocalypse Now* or *The Amityville Horror*, movies that frightened me so much I couldn't sleep at night.

Every weekend, we went to Third Street Jazz and Rock to buy records; then we walked down South Street to Jim's Steaks. Across the street at the Book Trader, we visited Bob Dickie and Jacy Webster, who played in the bands King of Siam, X Men, and, later, Strapping Fieldhands. We hung out in the store for hours, shooting the shit, talking music, books, art, and anything else we could think of.

Bob Dickie lived in a warehouse loft, the first living space like that I had ever seen. On the Fourth of July, Sheva, Lisa, Bob, and I climbed onto the roof of his building to watch the fireworks. On the way back down the dark and creepy stairs, Bob held my hand. We began dating, and stayed together all through that summer, even going to the shore one weekend. But Bob and I were very different. He was born at the Jersey Shore, but he couldn't swim. I loved the beach and the sun. He was arty and cultured; I was still finding my way. Bob was far more esoteric than I was. Our relationship ended by the fall.

Even though my musical tastes were focused on punk, I still appreciated other types of music. To this day, one of the best shows I ever saw in my

This is pretty heavy-handed with the eyeliner, even for me! Rikki Ercoli, an outstanding photographer, lived a few blocks away from me. RIKKI ERCOLI

life was James Brown at Ripley's on South Street. The Godfather of Soul brought the house down in one of the most impressive physical performances I have ever witnessed. As we were leaving, we discovered that while we were inside, a man showed up at the door claiming he was James Brown's son. When the bouncers wouldn't let him in, he pulled out a gun and shot up the sign at the bar next door. I was relieved I didn't know about this incident until after it was over.

My connection to Philly was deepening as I slowly but surely learned its streets, its culture, and its many quirks. I felt like I belonged, coexisting with thousands of people in a city with a symbiosis and synergy that fueled me every single day.

My Philadelphia apartment was located near 13th Street, a strip of porno theaters and peep shows, where a colorful cast of characters hung around day and night. DENISE MILUS

6
SAVAGE PINK

DESPITE ITS DANGEROUS, DIRTY, AND DERELICT FACADE, Philly was bursting with creativity and excitement everywhere—especially in its music, art, fashion, and nightlife. There was always something happening.

I was at Patti Brett's bar, Doobies—a shrine to David Bowie—when Tug McGraw struck out luckless Willie Wilson of the Kansas City Royals in the fall of 1980, handing the Phillies their first-ever World Series win. We all celebrated in the streets for three days. My brother Danny and his high school friends showed up for the parade. I bought them quarts of Olde English 800 malt liquor and promptly lost their group in the chaos. Afterward, they took the train back to Norristown on their own while I sweated over whether they were alive or dead, too petrified to call my mom to check on them.

Meanwhile, I worked every day at Cohen Shapiro and was a reliable and responsible employee. I knew every support staff job at the firm, and I worked as much overtime as possible so I could afford to keep up with the nightlife. Despite my work ethic, I constantly pushed the dress code at my job. My hair was very short, and I dyed it whiter than my natural blonde. I spiked it with Nu Nile and sprayed it with Aero Lak. Sometimes I dyed my hair pink or blue on the weekends, then dyed it back to blonde for work on Monday.

When I first started working at Cohen Shapiro, I wore dresses, skirts, suits, and heels. Now I wore pants and boots. Pants were not completely acceptable for women in the workplace at the time, and I was called into human resources about my attire on at least two occasions. "We have to remind you of the dress code," the office manager said. "Slacks are okay sometimes, but definitely not the corduroys and black Levi's you are wearing."

I didn't want to lose my job, so I complied as best I could, buying black pants at the Hit or Miss store near my apartment. It was so hard then to find pants that weren't made of spongy and uncomfortable polyester.

Pants or no pants, I was good at my job. I was always able to fill in for the receptionist, secretaries, telephone operator, or copy room clerk. I could type 120 words a minute, and my turnaround time on projects was ultrasonic. I was always on time and I never called in sick. Most of the lawyers liked me, and I made fast friends with the other girls in the word processing department. Carolyn and Tilly were only a year or two older than me, but they were smart and sophisticated. They clued me into the idiosyncrasies of each attorney. We had fun times together, sipping cocktails at lunch and dancing after work at Whispers, a nightclub a few blocks away from the law firm.

I tried to make myself valuable to the firm, so that even if I looked a little freaky to them, I could still keep my job. I liked having my own apartment and my own money. I found no romance or intrigue in squatting in a warehouse or starving in a garret. A safe place, a shower, and a working bathroom were all necessities for me.

My apartment building, the Adelphia House on Chestnut Street, was home to a menagerie of punks, artists, students, musicians, and writers. I met Kenny "Stinker" Gordon from Pure Hell, the groundbreaking and legendary Black punk band, in the lobby. Pure Hell was loud and fierce. They played shows with the Dead Boys and the Germs, and their single "These Boots Were Made for Walking" had hit number 4 on the UK alternative

Sadistic Exploits and I on the steps of my apartment building, Adelphia House. RIKKI ERCOLI

charts. They were the real deal. Kenny had an apartment on the fourth floor of my building. We hung out for a while, and even smooched once in the elevator. He told me about Pure Hell playing in England, and he gave me a cool pair of rock star sunglasses from London. I cried like a baby the day I realized I had left them on the subway.

I found kindred spirits everywhere in the city. Rikki Ercoli and Long Van Mai, a Vietnamese refugee punk with a keen fashion sense and a very private past, lived in a big old three-story apartment above Doc Johnson's Therapeutic Sexual Aids and Rubber Products at 1236 Arch Street, a few blocks from my apartment. Arch Street at the time was a seedy strip of mostly peep shows and porno theaters. The Greyhound bus terminal on the corner attracted a never-ending flow of vibrant characters. The entire area was grimy and lurid.

Rikki Ercoli was a talented photographer with a great eye. He shot photos of Sid Vicious, Patti Smith, Debbie Harry, and many other punk bands and icons. He took some dramatic black-and-white photos of me that I framed. Walking the four blocks between his apartment and mine was always treacherous. Once a guy grabbed my arm and tried to drag me toward a construction site. I had my little cassette boom box with me, and I whacked him on the side of the head with it as hard as I could. Then I raced down the street back to my apartment. I shudder to think what might have happened. I had nightmares about the experience for weeks, but I also realized I was developing skills that would keep me safe in the city.

Through Rikki, I met Johnny Vukich, whom I had long idolized since his days in the seminal Philly punk band the Autistics. Johnny was soft-spoken but bitingly sarcastic, and he always made me laugh. He was relentlessly cool and quite striking. Since I'd had a crush on him beginning in about 1977, I was elated to be able to hang around with him now.

Rikki also introduced me to the Ghoul Sisters, Marianne and Kathy, who taught me how to boldly wear blood-red lipstick without flinching. I had never worn lipstick before, and I soon realized its power. Red lipstick is potent, tough but feminine, and when I wore it, I felt confident and daring, like a superhero or femme fatale. The brand of lipstick the Ghoul Sisters gave me needed only to be applied once: it stained your lips and lasted all day.

❧

I wanted to get more involved in the music scene in some way. I needed to participate and give something back. I was pissed that I had zero musical talent, but I knew there had to be a way I could contribute. Writing for fanzines, managing a band, and promoting shows soon provided that opportunity.

On New Year's Eve 1981, I went to Omni's, and there I met Bryan and Peddrick. I had seen Peddrick around. He was a tough-looking punk rocker who played guitar. Bryan was a few days shy of eighteen and still in high school, but he was funny and smart and bore a more-than-passing resemblance to Billy Idol—then still the singer of Generation X. Bryan was a talented skateboarder as well. We met on the dance floor that night, and the three of us ended up staying up all night talking, then going to breakfast at the Midtown.

I was several years older than Bryan, but I fell fast. On our first date, we went to see *Quadrophenia*. We both loved it, and that sealed the deal. Bryan had a zest for life that I adored. He could make any situation fun.

Almost immediately, Bryan moved into my tiny apartment. Of course, my parents never knew this, or they would not have approved. But I was in love. Bryan got a job at Up Against the Wall, a trendy clothing store right next to the Adelphia House. When that closed, he started working at the Amazing Store, a little farther down the block. We spent hours playing pinball and *Pac-Man*, walking around Philly, eating cheese fries at Moriarty's, fish and chips at Arthur Treacher's Fish & Chips, and chicken wings at Chicken George. We took excursions to Penn's Landing and to South Street. I was having the time of my life in Philadelphia. I had a decent job, interesting friends, a cool boyfriend, and nearly every night I was able to enjoy the music I loved so much.

Bryan and Peddrick decided to form a band, and soon the Sadistic Exploits were born. I wasn't crazy about the name—it was probably a bit too sexualized for my ingrained Catholic school mores. Bryan came up with it. "I was watching TV one night long ago, and there was a show on called *Flops of 1980*, about all these shitty movies," Bryan said. "One of the movies was about a guy who was trying to break into a house to rape Kate Jackson [of *Charlie Angels'* fame], and he punched his hand through a door. Then they cut away and said the movie was 'nothing but a sadistic exploitation of women' and I said, 'That's the name.' Basically what it is, the name, is a reflection of the world around us. We're reflecting all the bullshit in the world."

We immediately created a stencil and spray-painted the band's name in red spray paint everywhere on the streets of Philadelphia. We wanted to create a buzz and make people ask who the Sadistic Exploits were. So we added the band's name to the crumbling walls of all the filthy, graffiti-painted lots filled with trash everywhere around us.

Bryan and Peddrick found Robbie to play bass. Robbie was handsome and sincere, and he had a ton of style. Eventually, the band recruited Miguel to play drums. He had sort of rockabilly-punk vibe and was also very cute. I wanted desperately to play a part in it all.

One day the guys approached me and asked if I wanted to be their manager. Did I ever. "Absolutely!" I told them. I eagerly agreed to pay a one-fifth share of expenses, including the rent for their practice space in Upper Darby, and, when it came time to make a record, the recording costs. Since the band members were frequently unemployed, I often found out I had to pitch in a little more. I never minded. I wanted to make things happen. I wanted to make a contribution.

One night at Omni's, I noticed some young women sitting in the front of the club. One had pink hair, one had blue hair, and one looked like a little Joan Jett. I was used to seeing regulars at Omni's. Most of us knew each other. I was anxious to know who these interesting-looking women were. Bryan and I introduced ourselves. Allison had the pink hair; KT, her girlfriend, had the blue hair; and Becky Wreck was the Jett. We learned that Becky played drums in a band called the Excuses. She looked like she was fourteen, but she was as tough as she was talented. These three women were smart, funny, and punk as fuck.

Allison and I especially became fast friends. She saw the world differently than I did, and I was anxious to be in her sphere. She opened up my mind to new ways of thinking about everything from gender roles to politics. We would have a couple of drinks together and laugh our asses off. We took our fun to the streets, tormenting the tourists riding in horse-drawn carriages around Philadelphia as we screamed: "Fucking bourgeois tourists! You have to have a poor animal pulling you around!" We snapped back with cutting comments at the jocks and disco dudes who tried to hit on us. And we were always right up front for every single show.

Allison started a fanzine called *Savage Pink*, focused on music with a little politics and social commentary on the side. I often contributed articles. I appreciated the opportunity to be able to express myself through language outside of the assigned exercises I had known from school. I'd cut my journalistic teeth writing the music column for my high school newspaper, expounding on bands like Queen and Kiss, so I had *some* technique and a decent command of grammar and punctuation. I recognized the power of words to communicate anger and joy and, of course, to change the world.

In August 1981, my friends Johnny, Robbie, Marianne, and I took the train to New York City to see the Misfits play at the Chase Park Lounge, a venue above a Chase Bank branch. We decided to stay at the notorious Chelsea Hotel, whose halls icons like Edie Sedgwick, Janis Joplin, and Patti Smith once prowled. We were unabashed punk tourists, taking photos in front of room 100, where Sid and Nancy lived and where Nancy was murdered in October 1978. The hotel was decrepit and there were cockroaches everywhere. We slept with the lights on, but that did little to deter the disgusting creatures.

Even Chase Park was loaded with cockroaches. I found one in my drink and another crawling on my chair. Despite this attack of creepy insects, seeing the Misfits for the first time was an incredible experience. The club wasn't that crowded, and we were able to get right up front. Glenn Danzig was an impressive front man with a strong voice and magnetic stage presence, and the band's songs had a sing-along quality that made the experience feel participatory. Back then, it was actually kind of uncool to like the Misfits. Their makeup and horror film imagery didn't play well with the stripped-down aesthetic of most punk bands. But I loved their melodic tunes and the way they sang about Marilyn Monroe and ghouls and fiends. I liked that they dressed up and wore makeup—they reminded me of my glam rock days.

Overleaf: *Jumping for joy! Bryan and I punking it up, Summer of 1981.* JEANNE LASORDA

With my best friend, Allison Schnackenberg, at CBGB in 1981.
COURTESY OF ALLISON SCHNACKENBERG

PUNKING IT UP IN THE BIG CITY

LOCATED PERFECTLY MIDWAY between New York and Washington, DC, Philly became a regular and much-anticipated stop for touring punk bands. Between major visits by marquee names, the city also had local acts playing in bars and clubs nearly every night of the week. Live music was everywhere. In 1981, there was always a show happening, somewhere for us to go.

Around this same time, more and more punk music was being made by females or female-fronted bands like Siouxsie and the Banshees, Vice Squad, the Slits, X-Ray Spex, and even Girlschool—who were considered more metal than punk, but I still loved them. My absolute favorite songs at this time were the Avengers' "The American in Me" and "We are the One." I loved Penelope Houston's voice, and I blasted those songs nonstop, singing along at the top of my lungs.

I loved the fact that many of our Philadelphia bands had female musicians. Becky Wreck played drums and Lisa Mauro was the vocalist for the Excuses. While I never saw them play live, their legend continued for a long time. Becky was an intensely talented drummer, and Lisa was tough, sexy, and one of the most confident women I had ever met. In the Stickmen, the enigmatic, inventive genius Beth Ann Lejman played trumpet, organ, keyboards, and guitar. The band's sound defied convention. Their fascinating blend of art, synthesizers, and guitar was confusing to me because it fit no

Top photo: *I wanted to be a contributor, but I couldn't play an instrument or sing, so I was thrilled when the Sadistic Exploits asked me to manage them.* LISA HAUN

known genre, and they opened my mind to new forms of music.

The art band Head Cheese was almost entirely comprised of women banging on plastic containers and speaking their lyrics. I was envious that these women had the guts to stand on a stage and present their percussive noise and voices to the world.

One night, Beth Ann Lejman and my high school friend Isabella led eight screaming women and twelve drummers in loincloths through the Philadelphia subway in a piece they called "The Wild Women of Wongo." I knew nothing about performance art at the time, but I respected and was in awe of Beth Ann's innovation and brilliance.

Years later, two out-of-touch academics, Kevin Egan and Maren Larsen, denigrated the women who made up the infrastructure of the Philly punk scene in an article for Drexel University titled "Philly Punk: Gender Politics in the City of Brotherly Love." They stated: "The level of involvement [of women] seemed to be more often confined to working behind the scenes, and, perhaps, being part of the crowd." This sort of "invisible labor," they said, "characterizes the performance of femininity as caretaker and nurturer. Women worked in the shadows, maintaining the infrastructure of a punk scene that allowed a predominantly masculine majority of musicians to perform publicly. In this sense, masculine performance was granted a public persona, while feminine performance operated privately to uphold that public sphere."

Of course, I was outraged by that article. I never saw the scene that way. I was always keenly aware and appreciative of the people, whether male or female, who worked to bring music to others via the music scene—and not just the punk underworld. Eagan and Larsen, however, relegated women to "the shadows" when in fact we were up front, literally, physically, and symbolically, as integral, important, and necessary orchestrators of the scene. Demeaning the work by dismissing it as "women's work" and "invisible labor" was a blatant attempt to advance a thesis that only reaffirmed the patriarchal status of men.

I could tell that the authors had done limited research. If they had looked even a little deeper, they would have uncovered the many women who performed in Philadelphia punk bands. Instead, they marginalized and disparaged the women who helped build the framework of punk and proclaimed our work trivial. Egan and Larsen's careless and poorly researched article was a disgrace and, as an educator today, I would not have accepted that kind of sloppy work from a fourteen-year-old. Their off-base generalizations offended me as a woman, an educator, and a punk.

For me as a female who for most of her life had been told what to do, how to act, and what to think, punk was incredibly liberating. I always thought that exploring nonconformity and being on the cusp of something new was exciting and compelling. Punk helped me feel like a total badass. I didn't care what anyone else thought about me or the music I loved.

❦

I soon had my hands full, managing the Exploits, attending practices and booking them at clubs like Omni's. People began calling me Nancy Exploit. As someone who never had a nickname before—other than "Hey, Blondie!"—I was psyched. We put out a little fanzine, and my photo was included alongside that of the band members. I felt like a member of something unique. I had found my clan within my punk tribe.

The Exploits recorded their first single in November 1981 at Caruso Sound in Upper Darby. It featured the songs "Anarchy" and "Freedom." The band asked me to write a piece for the inside cover. They wanted something that reflected their political views, which focused strongly on the right to dissent of Americans. However, as I started to write, I felt frustrated because I was ignorant and uneducated about politics. Basically, everything I knew I'd gleaned from bands like the Clash, Crass, or the Dead Kennedys. So I spent hours in the Philadelphia Public Library reading John Locke, Henry David Thoreau, and Hannah Arendt. These philosophers were all new to me. I hadn't studied them in school. At that moment I vowed to eventually go back to school and continue my education, so I could understand more

about what was happening in the world.

Having a record available meant the Exploits could now try to get gigs outside of Philadelphia. I wanted to see the band play out of state, even though we didn't have transportation. I assembled press kits by hand and sent them to clubs to get bookings. New York City seemed like a first logical stop. I was thrilled to get a slot at A7, a tiny venue on the corner of East Seventh Street and Avenue A in the East Village, opening for the Mob, the band formed by Jack Flanagan of Heart Attack after he saw the Bad Brains and decided to play louder and faster music.

I also called Hilly Kristal at CBGB and begged him for a show. Every time I called, he would say, "Call me back next week," or, "Call me tomorrow morning." And I always did. I was relentless.

Finally, I wore Hilly down, and he gave the band a show—that was the kind of guy Hilly was. He gave everyone a chance.

I'm not sure how we got the equipment to New York City, but those shows at CBGB and A7 are some of my fondest memories. We played with bands like the False Prophets, the Misguided, and Reagan Youth. I quickly made friends with New York City punks like John Watson, who soon became the first singer of Agnostic Front; Jimmy G., who went on to sing for the Cavity Creeps and then Murphy's Law; and the easygoing and hilarious Chris Charucki, who sang for Cause for Alarm.

John Watson was and still is, by far, one of the coolest individuals I have ever met. He had a style all his own, and he was always so sweet. Watching John on the dance floor was always captivating—there was something about the way he moved that was at once both fluid and powerful. Jimmy G. was probably about sixteen back then, and he was exuberantly happy. He could latch onto a phrase and make it part of the punk lexicon. As far as I'm concerned, he can take the credit for popularizing "mosh it up," a phrase first used by the Bad Brains but taken to the next level by Jimmy.

Besides Jimmy, Chris, and John, the iconic crew of New York punks at CBGB, A7, and 171A included Alex Kinon from Cause for Alarm and his sharp girlfriend Linda; the adorable Bubby, from Russia; Louie Rivera from Antidote, who wore prescription sunglasses day and night, inside and outside; Michelle, the first woman I knew to fully shave her head; the ever-protective Frenchy; the gorgeous Blue, and the lovely, soft-spoken Robbie Cryptcrash. Harley Flanagan, the drummer for the Stimulators who went on to start the Cro-Mags, was an obnoxious little teenager who chased me and tried to throw ice cubes down my shirt.

The Exploits and I adored Jack and Ralph and all the guys in the Mob and played shows with them often. I enjoyed going to New York, and I loved the bands I saw there like the Young and the Useless, Kraut, and one of my all-time favorites, Crucial Truth, a group of Florida transplants. The Amtrak train to New York was fast and fairly cheap, and even though New York City was a seriously scary place in the early '80s, I frequently made the trek, either by myself or in the company of a few friends. We traveled to Penn Station in midtown, headed down to the Bowery, and then ended up leaving CBGB or A7 or 171A at three o'clock in the morning. We'd have

At CBGB around 1981, with roughly fifteen-year-old Harley Flanagan popping bubble gum.
ALLISON SCHNACKENBERG

to wait for the early-morning train back to Philly. The police wouldn't let us sleep in the station; if we tried, they'd bang their nightsticks *hard* right next to our heads and yell, "Wake up!" It was also impossible to go to the bathroom in Penn Station because nearly every stall housed a person who had made that spot their home.

In general, the area around Penn Station and Times Square was squalid and perilous. This was not Mayor Giuliani's Disney World Times Square; this was the Times Square of *Taxi Driver*. In fact, 1981 was New York City's most crime-ridden year to date, and it seemed that danger lurked everywhere. But we were fearless and felt protected by our youth and our punkness.

The women in New York were a special breed. They came from varied backgrounds, but they knew how to have fun and get out of a jam. Lazar was one of the first women I met. She was tiny but wiry and filled with nervous energy. She was often my partner in crime during my New York adventures. Lazar was bold and daring. One night she and I went to the bodega near 171A to get an Orange Crush. When we came back around the corner, we saw the cops arresting kids in front of the venue. 171A was not zoned as a club, and it did not have a liquor license. "Shit, what should we do?" she asked.

"Well, maybe if they had something else more pressing to focus on, they'd leave the kids alone," I reasoned. Lazar picked up the phone and dialed 911 to report an imaginary but heinous crime a few blocks away from the club. In seconds, the cops let all the kids go and sped away. Everyone bought us beers the rest of the night.

Of course, the Bowery and the Lower East Side were a war zone. At CBGB one evening, Allison and I had to pee terribly, but the doorless bathrooms downstairs were notoriously disgusting. We decided peeing outside might be a better option. We found some stairs that led to an underground basement apartment. Since the building looked abandoned, we figured this would be a good, private spot. Unfortunately, we picked a part of the Hells Angels clubhouse, and bikers came running out. I screamed to Allison, "Run!" and we ran like hell, but thankfully they didn't chase us more than a block. I'm sure they assessed our threat and dismissed it. They had to have known we were headed back to CB's.

❧

Philly was a dangerous place, too, in the early 1980s. Much of the city was blighted, with abandoned and boarded-up buildings everywhere, even on touristy South Street. Cockroaches scurried down the street faster than I could. Rats and vermin were everywhere. Once I was making a call in a telephone booth when a huge, greasy rat ran under the door. I screamed like a lunatic, trying to get the door open. Thank God I had on boots, because the rat was just as scared as me, and he was biting at everything. Punk fashion is nothing if not practical.

At the time, Philly had a militant and heavy-handed mayor and was home to the only major police department in America to have been investigated for corruption by the US Justice Department. The Philly police force did *not* like punks. One time, Bryan and I were spray-painting the Sadistic Exploits stencil on the street, and a cop came at us like he had caught us desecrating the Liberty Bell. He ripped the stencil from our hands, tore it to pieces, and screamed in our faces, spitting everywhere. I was scared shitless, but luckily the cop let us go as soon as another call came over his radio.

Another time while I was coming back from a party in New Jersey, my magnetic transit card wouldn't work in the turnstile. I wasn't about to miss my train and wait an hour for another, so I hopped over the turnstile. Someone must have alerted Philly police. When I pulled into the Ninth and Locust Street station in Philly, the cops were waiting, and they set their K-9 dogs on me like I was some sort of escaped convict.

"Look, I have a card!" I yelled, waving it at them, while a snarling dog's teeth snapped at my pant leg.

One of the smarmy cops sneered, and said, "You know, you'd be pretty if you didn't have that fucked-up hair." They let me go.

Yet another time, my friend John, drummer for the New Jersey band Autistic Behavior, and I were leaving the East Side Club, situated on the very street where I lived. Suddenly, police cars surrounded us, and plainclothes cops right out of a *Starsky & Hutch* episode stepped out of the shadows with their guns pointed in our faces.

"We have a report of terrorist activity," they informed us.

"By who? Us?" I asked incredulously. I was quivering.

We knew better than to argue with Philly's men in blue. The cops searched both of us. I was wearing a Boy of London jacket that was covered with zippers. The police took *forever* to go through each pocket, while I was shaking and near tears. I have no idea who or what they were looking for—maybe another pair of terrorist punks—but they eventually got back in their cars and let us go.

Except for the police, most of the folks in Center City Philly truly accepted the punks who lived there. It was, after all, the City of Brotherly Love, and it took a lot to shock or frighten most Philadelphians. They were

Acting out the typical cop-punk dynamic (with the help of a friend on the force).

used to colorful characters in their midst. I did experience catcalls and yells of "Hey, Blondie!" when I walked down the street. When Rick James's song "Super Freak" came out, random guys sang it to me. That usually made me laugh. Sometimes I felt safer alone, as long as the harassment was limited to catcalls and not dragging me into vacant lots. When we punks walked in groups in the early 1980s, people often tried to start fights with us.

Running into other punks around Philly was fun, though. We were a small group, easily discernible by our clothing, the pins on our jackets, and our hair—or lack thereof. Seeing a stranger with any distinguishing punk features could lead to a long conversation because the music made us kindred spirits. For example, I first met Jim McMonagle from Flag of Democracy after seeing *Mad Max* at a theater on Chestnut Street. Jim's friend Cheryl had just shaved his head, and I excitedly ran up to them saying, "Cool! Philly skinheads!" (In those days in the US, having a shaved head was associated with nothing more nefarious than a love of punk and hardcore music.) We became instant friends over a feast at Roy Rogers, while the workers jumped on the Rick James bandwagon, calling us "super freaks."

As a punk, I never felt that I was weird or a misfit because I didn't conform to what everyone else was doing. Quite the contrary. I didn't want to be like everyone else. There was no fun in that. I wanted to be different. If other people didn't understand it, I figured it was because they were too closed-minded—or too boring.

Often my friends and I would walk by throngs of tourists at the Liberty Bell or Independence Hall, and the out-of-towners would run up to us, asking, "Can we take your photo?" If they were particularly obnoxious, we'd charge them five bucks. At that time, punk was still a relatively new phenomenon, and people weren't used to seeing kids with dyed hair or Mohawks dressed the way we were. Even so, I felt increasingly at home in Philly. I loved the city's rich history.

When I was growing up, my maternal grandmother would often tell us that we were direct descendants of Benjamin Franklin. I assumed this was one of those family myths passed down from generation to generation. But one day, many years later, my mother and I were hiking near an old graveyard. "Some of our ancestors are buried here," my mother pointed out.

We found their graves, and I noticed many of our deceased relatives had the middle name Franklin. I said to my mother, "Wouldn't it be cool if we really *were* related to Franklin? Let's find out!" So we hired a genealogist from the Historical Society of Philadelphia to do the research. After about a year of investigation, much to our surprise, we discovered my grandmother's story was true: I was an eighth-generation grandchild to Benjamin Franklin directly descended from his daughter, Sally.

Since I was a child, Ben Franklin had always been my favorite "founding father." I liked that even though he made well-documented mistakes, he always tried to be a good person. I often turned to him for inspiration and advice. Franklin didn't hesitate to oppose powerful figures when he witnessed injustice or arbitrary abuse of authority. His rebelliousness was legendary. It's no wonder I felt his spirit when I walked the streets of Philadelphia each day.

Living in Philly could be expensive, and money still remained an issue. I sold my heavy gold Bishop Kenrick class ring to help finance the Sadistic Exploits' first recording. I think I got seventy dollars for it. But at that time in my life, high school wasn't really a fond memory, so I felt no remorse or real loss. If I ran out of money a few days before payday, we would go to the Crystal Tea Room at John Wanamaker, and I'd use my Wanamaker's charge card to buy lunch. We could feast on tuna melts and fancy salads. The other patrons—usually women lunching or uptight mother-and-daughter pairs— would stare at us, appalled at our spiky hair and unconventional clothing. Other times, I charged cheese and pepperoni gift boxes at Gimbels or candy at Strawbridge & Clothier. When the lawyers at my job had a big luncheon, the support staff got to take the leftover sandwiches home, and I'd always get in on that, too. No one ever starved. I knew how to be resourceful.

The gearhead. Funny photos—considering that I've never had a driver's license. RIKKI ERCOLI

8
BLACK FLAG, S.O.A., AND THE KENSINGTON BRAWL

DURING THE SUMMER OF 1981, I booked the Sadistic Exploits a show with West Coast trailblazers Black Flag at City Gardens in Trenton, New Jersey. Black Flag was one of the first hardcore punk bands to get in a van and drive across the country. The stories said they were being harassed by the police in L.A. and figured it was a good time to get out of town. We were dying to see the band that hammered the authorities and their audiences into such a frenzy.

City Gardens was a rock and punk mecca, but the club had a terrible reputation. I heard a story about a girl who went there for a show, was kidnapped by a biker gang, and came back with a tattoo over her lip that said "Eat Me." Sure, I embraced my new punk identity, but part of me was still a Catholic suburban schoolgirl from Norristown.

Mortal dangers aside, City Gardens was a great place to see a show. The stage was huge and high. The Exploits were about to be exposed to a whole new audience of New Jerseyites. We could only hope they'd be as open and receptive as our Philly crowds.

Black Flag's dark and menacing reputation was at least as intimidating as the club's. Our friends from the New Jersey band Autistic Behavior talked about Black Flag a lot. The ABs, as we called them, had formed when three of them met at Great Adventure amusement park, which I thought was hilarious. I loved the ABs as a band and as people. On their recommendation, I bought Black Flag's first EP, *Nervous Breakdown*, and then their five-song *Jealous Again* EP, and I played them constantly.

Around this time I first began to see a distinction between punk and what was now being called "hardcore." US bands mostly played hardcore, which was clearly something different. I liked the harder vibe and the physicality, and I began to lean that way in my musical preferences. Not all my friends felt the same; several of my female friends gave me a hard time. "C'mon," they said. "Hardcore is a boys' club. Is that really what you want?"

There were certainly fewer women involved with hardcore than with punk, but hardcore spoke better to the anger, frustration, and resentment I carried inside me. I didn't care what anyone else said. I felt welcome in the hardcore world—much more than I did in "normal" society. "Boys' club" or not, I felt more acceptance from the guys in hardcore than I did from most women in the regular world outside the music scene.

Every time the Exploits played live, they showed themselves growing tighter, and the evening with Black Flag at City Gardens was no exception. I tried to see the band through the eyes of the first-time audience members. Even though Black Flag was the main attraction that evening, the Exploits' energy onstage was contagious—kids slam-danced and stage dived with total abandon. Afterward, we all jumped into the crowd to await Black Flag. Dez Cadena was Black Flag's singer in early 1981, and his raw voice led the charge through a primal performance that created an insane energy.

Toward the end of Black Flag's set, Bryan slipped on some beer, fell to the ground, and was kicked in the head. We carted him off to the hospital, where we were told he had a hairline fracture of the skull. The doctors sent us home with instructions to wake him up every hour to be sure he didn't lapse into a coma or die. Somehow, we took incidents like this in stride. Someone was always getting kicked in the head or smashed in the face. A trip to the emergency room was often part of the evening's itinerary.

❦

A few weeks after the City Gardens show, on July 10, 1981, we went to see Black Flag play again—this time with Autistic Behavior and DC favorites S.O.A. at the Starlite Ballroom. The club was in Kensington, a tough, working-class area just a short el-train ride from downtown Philly. David Carroll from the Hot Club was booking the Starlite. The venue was great, the bands would be great; this time the neighborhood was the problem.

I had seen a show or two at the Starlite without incident, but my friend Mike Condi from the Proteens once had a terrible experience there. His band was invited to play the venue, so one night beforehand Mike; John Marconi, whom we called Marcus Hook; Chris Spadafora, also known as Spanarkle; and Tommy Ajax decided to check it out when the Ben Wah Torpedos and Warm Jets were performing with some other bands. "It was extra tense inside the venue, but nothing but a few scuffles occurred," he told me. Afterward, as Mike and his bandmates walked to their car, they were attacked by a gang of fifty locals.

"I was hit in the back of the head and knocked unconscious—for how long I don't know," Mike said. "The street around the club was crumbling, and the locals were taking chunks of it and smashing it through our car windshield." Then the Proteens bassist Marcus was ripped out of the car and pummeled. Spanarkle sped away, clipping one of the assailants with his car.

When Mike regained consciousness, he found Marcus. Beaten and bloodied, the two wandered the streets of Kensington, trying to figure out a way home.

"A Vietnam vet with no legs saw us, and he knew something wasn't right," remembers Mike. "He hid us out in his one-room apartment for about an hour, then he gave us all the money he could spare—a handful of change. We didn't even have enough for the el-train ride, but when we arrived at the station, the conductor saw what shape we were in and took mercy on us. He let us ride, anyway That whole experience was a real nightmare."

I should have more closely heeded the warning of Mike's story, but I wanted to see S.O.A. and Black Flag. The event would be special, as S.O.A. singer Henry Garfield was about to adopt the name Rollins and become the new singer of Black Flag. But when the night finally arrived, I walked into the Starlite and immediately felt a prickly and totally unfamiliar tension. Something wasn't right.

Lots of hardcore kids from Washington, DC, were at this show to support what would be S.O.A.'s last show. The DC bands represented a unique and very young faction of hardcore. S.O.A. and their friends Minor Threat were part of a contingent of kids who weren't into alcohol or drugs. Their lyrics often reflected that stance. In their song "Straight Edge," Minor Threat coined a term that would eventually be used universally to describe an alcohol- and drug-free lifestyle. They were used to their outsider status, and used to fighting to defend themselves or just settle their differences.

Not all the DC kids followed the straight edge philosophy, judging by their self-admittedly drunken behavior at the Starlite. Minor Threat singer Ian MacKaye was among those kids who had traveled up from DC. "That Kensington show—what a mess," he says. "That night was so fraught. Things started popping off between DC and Philly punks. I don't remember anyone talking about going up there to tangle with the local kids, but it was an era in which that sort of thing happened. I didn't have any beef with the Philly punks and wasn't involved with what was happening on the dance floor. All I know is that people started fighting, and I was bugged because I knew that some of the DC people who were kicking things off were really drunk, and I thought that they were being dicks."

Meanwhile, the Starlite was also filling up with local Kensington kids, and they did not look pleased at the sight of a bunch of weird punks from DC and Philly invading their neighborhood. When the bands began, the locals were first amused by the slamming in the pit; then several of them jumped in, taking cheap shots. The punks, meanwhile, gave it right back, elbow for elbow, until the pressure in the room soon became stifling.

I barely recall seeing Black Flag play. Henry sang a few songs with them, and I wasn't sure how I felt about that. I still liked Dez, who was now playing guitar. Something about Henry was very intense, though. If there was going to be a fight that night, I was glad he was there and on our side.

The next thing I knew, fists were flying, and bottles were hurtling through the air. The Kensington kids didn't differentiate between the Philly punks and the DC punks; the DC kids didn't distinguish between the Philly punks and the Philly locals, so the brawl erupted into total mayhem. At one point, a big, skinhead Neanderthal from DC walked up and looked me right in the eyes. I stood up to him, not expecting him to do anything—but he punched me right in the face. I hit the ground and blacked out for a few seconds.

I always carried Mace with me, and I figured this was the time to use it. I crawled to my feet and maced anyone who came near me. Then I ran for the door. I found my friends, and we hid on the street, crouching between cars while we listened for the rumbling of the next elevated train to arrive. My head was aching. I wondered how I'd ended up in this real-life scene straight from the street gang movie *The Warriors*. I prayed silently, making deals with God: "Get me out of this alive, and I'll never leave the house again. Save my ass and I'll go back to college and become a lawyer."

As Ian MacKaye recalls: "A bunch of DC people, maybe fifteen or twenty in a half-dozen cars, had gone up to see Black Flag and Henry's last S.O.A. show before he left to join Black Flag. The first thing that probably should have warned us away from the trip was that my car started dying on the drive up. I had a 1970 Plymouth Duster, and apparently something was going screwy with the electrical system, because it kept stalling.

"When we finally made it to Philadelphia, and more specifically the Kensington neighborhood, I remember thinking, 'This is a really weird place.' Coming from DC, we had never encountered a 'bad' white neighborhood, so we had no understanding of where we were. The Starlite Ballroom was on a street that was under some sort of underpass; to us it looked like a movie set, with old men in sleeveless undershirts sitting on stoops giving us the stink eye."

During the melee inside the show, Ian recalls some smaller local neighborhood kids coming inside, taking a shot at a DC kid, and then immediately running out of the venue. Ian recognized a setup when he saw one. As the rest of the DC people chased after the kids, Ian started to yell: "Don't go outside!"

"I ran down the stairs," he says, "to the lobby area on the first floor to try to head people off at the pass. But they were in hot pursuit and just ran past me and out the door of the venue. When they were about half a block down the street, a bunch of bigger local dudes with bats and other weapons came out of the alley between the DC kids and the venue. This meant that some people had to make a choice: to either run deeper into the neighborhood or turn around and try to run through the gauntlet.

"The DC guys were fighters, and they could hold their own, but it got crazy. These local guys had pipes and bricks, and they were beating the shit out of people. Even the old men were throwing rocks at us. It was essentially a riot, and it didn't take long for the cops to show up. They came in a number of cars and parked down the middle of the street to create a wall between the opposing forces, but that didn't stop some of the Kensington kids from running through the line and attacking DC kids. They didn't give a shit!"

Finally, there was a standoff as the police managed to make a line dividing the punks and the Kensington kids. The cops announced they would leave in ten minutes. "So we all started piling into our cars to make our exit," says Ian, "but when I turned the key in my car, *nothing*. My alternator had completely died, and I had no power whatsoever. All of the other cars had gone, and it was just me and few other DC kids sitting there in a dead car with the Kensington toughs waiting for the cops to leave."

One of many black eyes that year. With Adam Bomb from Philly's Decontrol.

Ian and the DC kids reasoned with the police, who gave him a jump start so he was able to get the car away from the Starlite and back on the highway home. "The tape deck was starting to run slower and slower," he says, "and the headlights were starting to dim, and it was clear that the car wasn't going to make it back to DC that night—but I was elated just to have escaped from Kensington!"

My own prayers were answered after what seemed like an eternity, when I heard the el rumble into the station, and my group of Philly punks was able to dash up the stairs and jump aboard without being killed. Thankfully, we were unscathed, except for some bumps and bruises.

A few years later, I read an account of that show by the late John Stabb of DC's Government Issue. He listed his friends' injuries: Jaimie, who used to play in Iron Cross, got twenty-two stitches as a result of a baseball bat to the head; Bert from Youth Brigade was slashed across the back; Eric from Red C took a lead pipe to the face; and Mike from Law and Order was beaten in the head with a billy club.

Stabb took his injured friends to the emergency room. They were covered in blood and "scared shitless." While they were waiting to be seen, a guy came in holding a wad of tissues to his throat. When Stabb asked him what happened, the man took the tissues away, revealing a big chunk of meat missing from his gullet. He said he had gotten in a bar brawl, and the other guy couldn't fight, so he took a bite out of his opponent's throat instead. "Jesus Christ, man, Philly is for barbarians!" Stabb concluded.

I returned to work that Monday sporting a huge black eye. My coworkers Tilly and Carolyn barraged me with questions: "Girl, what the hell happened to you? Are you okay? Can you see? Should you even be at work right now?" I told them about the brawl. They shook their heads in disbelief. "What could possibly be fun about that?" they asked.

Despite the chaos—and the risk of injury—it was impossible to explain how I felt at home at a show with my friends; it was too difficult to explain the exhilaration I experienced when I saw a band I loved.

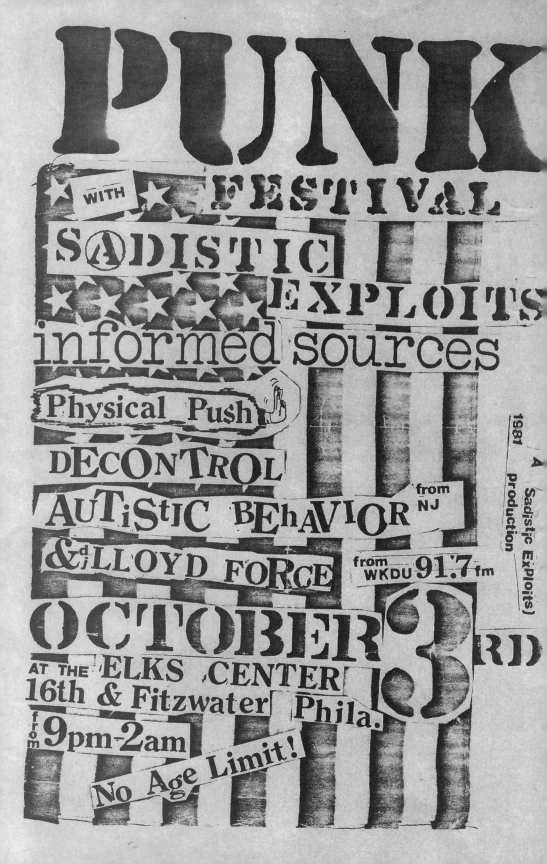

9

PUNK FEST AND
THE ANTI-PASTI DRAMA

I CONTINUED TO BOOK GIGS FOR THE SADISTIC EXPLOITS, and their following grew in Philly, New Jersey, and New York. The band even played a frat party once; the pay was fifty dollars and a beer ball—a dark brown plastic globe filled with five gallons of beer.

That September 1981, the Exploits were offered the opening slot for X at Ripley Music Hall on South Street. Ripley's was a great venue—not at all like what we were used to playing. I mean, James Brown had performed there! The band even had a real dressing room. I was excited to see X, especially because their singer Exene Cervenka was another idol of mine. She was a punk legend, not just as a musician, but as a writer and a style pioneer.

The previous month, August 1981, my neighborhood punk club Omni's had burned down and been turned into a parking lot. But I was lucky. The East Side Club, located right in the basement of my apartment building, changed their format from disco to punk rock. This was an incredible new development. What could be better than having a punk club in my own basement? I could hang out there every night, but come home to use my own bathroom if I wanted. We could drink in my house between bands instead of paying for expensive cocktails at the bar! The future looked bright.

The East Side Club was anxious to draw crowds, so first thing they gave free VIP cards to all the punks. Bobby Startup worked as the DJ there and booked the bands. He was a bit of a legend in Philadelphia from working at the Hot Club. Also, he and Lee Paris had been instrumental in bringing punk to the city in the late 1970s. In the past, Bobby had managed bands like the Bloodless Pharaohs, Brian Setzer's art/new wave band that reminded me of Roxy Music mixed with the Talking Heads, and then later the Stray Cats. I looked up to Bobby, and he opened the doors at his new club to the Exploits for a few shows, including one with San Francisco's female-fronted punk band UXA.

But you still had to be twenty-one or older to get into the East Side Club. After meeting the DC kids, and feeling the surge of hardcore and the more youthful faction of punks, the Exploits and I wanted to reach a larger, all-ages audience. Options were limited. Out-of-town bands almost always played twenty-one-and-over clubs. So if a band wasn't playing an arena or a concert setting like the Tower Theater, anyone under twenty-one had scarce opportunities to see live music. We realized that if we wanted the Sadistic Exploits to reach an all-ages audience, we would have to make it happen ourselves.

I remembered when Lee Paris and cohorts had rented their own spooky and atmospheric venue to put on a Bauhaus concert in 1980. "How about we rent the Elks Center to do a show?" I suggested. Everyone agreed that would be a great spot.

"It should be a punk festival!" Bryan exclaimed. "We'll call it 'Punk Fest I' because we'll be sure to do more. It could be the first of many."

"And we'll just feature local bands!" Robbie added. We all nodded.

We had no blueprint for a do-it-yourself festival. We knew we wanted good bands to play, and we knew we'd have to advertise heavily. Next we realized one of our biggest expenses would be renting a big PA—a public address system with microphones, a mixer, amplifiers, and speakers. As we researched the next step, we learned that we would unfortunately have to pay for all of this up front. But we methodically ticked off each part of our plan to make the show a reality.

One of the bands we knew we wanted on the bill was Informed Sources. Frank Blank from Omni's had hooked up with the intimidating Brian Lee and Northeast Philly's Joe Stack to start the band. I remember being a little frightened of Brian. He was tough—he sported a safety pin in his cheek that connected to his ear. I had only seen that look in photos of punks from England. I adored Joe. He had spiky blond hair and wore a leather jacket every single day, no matter the weather. Inside, he was pure sweetness. Every band in Philly struggled to find a drummer, but eventually Informed Sources added Doug Mosko to the mix. His brother, Bill, worked at Third Street Jazz and Rock.

We also invited the power trio Decontrol; Adam Avery, Richie Birch, and Keith "Keeth" Lenderman made up one of the tightest and most entertaining bands playing Philly. Keeth had actually played drums on the Sadistic Exploits single before Miguel mastered the songs. Then we rounded off the show with Physical Push and our friends Autistic Behavior. All of these bands represented one facet or another of the Philly punk scene, interconnected, yet unique in their own ways. Besides the Exploits, I had only seen Autistic Behavior play once before—at the Black Flag/S.O.A. show that ended in a riot. I barely remembered their performance. It was just important for us to give young local punks a chance to perform for the kids who needed to see them most.

We wanted everyone to know about the show, so we created a cool flyer that got people's attention. Bryan had a sharp artistic eye, so he designed the flyer, which featured the word PUNK in two-inch stencil-lettering at the top, followed by the smaller FESTIVAL written below. He superimposed each band's unique name logo over an American flag. Luckily, I had access to a copy machine at my job. Bryan and I snuck into the building after hours and ran off hundreds of flyers for the show. Then the Exploits and I set out all over the city wheat-pasting flyers everywhere.

Wheat-pasting was a nasty job: you filled a bucket with the wheat-paste glue mixture and water, and then slathered it over the flyer with a paintbrush. The slop always ended up all over your clothes, on your face, and in your hair. We pasted flyers on telephone poles, streetlights, traffic signals, boarded-up storefronts, and abandoned buildings. We went out for three nights straight and blanketed the city with flyers. There were very few spots in Philly that didn't boast a Punk Fest flyer. We also hung up flyers in Third Street, and at Plastic Fantastic, another cool record store in Ardmore.

We decided that admission would be five dollars; we thought five bands for five dollars was a great deal.

"Do you think anyone will come?" I asked the guys. "I mean, don't we already know the fifty or so punks in the Philadelphia area? And will *they* even show up?" We had no idea.

My little brother Danny was barely out of high school, but I called him at home. "I need someone to work the door at the show. Someone I can trust. Do you think you can handle it?"

"What do you think?" he said. He was in. We were *all* in.

I knew nothing about a public address system, so Bryan and Peddrick took care of renting that. We wanted to have enough power to do the bands justice. I'm not sure where we got the two-hundred-dollar rental fee for the equipment. Maybe we saved it from sales of singles, or what the Exploits made from playing shows—otherwise, I might have fronted it from my meager savings account.

As the date grew near, we worried about the Elks. The building we were using for the show belonged to the Improved Benevolent Protective Order of Elks of the World (IBPOEW), established in 1897 as an African American fraternal order modeled on the Benevolent and Protective Order of the Elks, a white established fraternal order that refused admission to Black people. These Elks had a long-standing history of providing a space for the community. Jazz bands played the venue in the 1940s, but we had no idea what the Elks would think of our punk festival. Even though the show

My brother Danny—someone I could trust with the money—and I at Punk Fest. RIKKI ERCOLI

was all ages, there was a bar downstairs where people could buy cheap drinks. The Elks regulars, many of them the age of our grandparents, would be down there socializing with the punks. What would they think about these freaky-looking kids and this loud music? Would they change their minds about letting us rent their hall, and throw us all out on the night of the show?

❦

Punk Fest I took place on a beautiful fall day in October 1981. I borrowed a vintage black lace dress from my friend Allison. I paired it with black engineer boots and fishnets and felt ready to be a sort of unofficial master of ceremonies. Allison was psyched, too. She set up a table in the foyer of the Elks so she could sell and promote her *Savage Pink* magazine.

Within minutes of the doors opening, a large line formed, and colorfully dressed people of all ages started to stream into the Elks. I had no idea where all these people came from, but there were hundreds of them. Robbie stood next to me and said, "What the fuck? Who are all these people?" I was shocked and elated. My brother Danny had to keep running to the bathroom to stuff the entrance money into his secure money belt. We were definitely not in a good neighborhood, and no way could we afford to be robbed.

Looking back, I'm surprised how well organized we were. Before the show, each band received a typewritten "Agenda for Bands Participating in Punk Fest," which included strict guidelines for load-in time, playing time, and guest list protocol. I was anxious about bands playing over their time limit—and about the cops shutting down the show.

I ran up and down the stairs and through the backstage all night, trying to ensure that everything went smoothly. The band Physical Push canceled at the last minute. I wasn't too concerned about that, because the other bands would have more time to play. Informed Sources opened the night and it was their first show. Frank ripped into the intro to "Pretty Vacant," and it sounded awesome until everything went silent. I freaked out. If the PA conked out, we had no show. People ran onto the stage to help, but they couldn't figure out what was wrong: the amp was on, but there was no sound. After about a minute (although it seemed so much longer), someone discovered the end of a cord had dislodged from its connection by about an eighth of an inch. "It just needed a gentle push back in," Frank told me.

Adam from Decontrol remembers being especially anxious to play Punk Fest I. "Being in one of the few punk bands in Philly was kind of a lonely thing. Most people despised us or our kind. The Philly punk scene was often literally underground—we mostly played sparsely attended dark basement parties. At Punk Fest, we suddenly found ourselves in front of a large, enthusiastic audience for the first time. We nervously played our hearts out, made lots of new friends, and gained fans. There was an electricity in the air that recharged us, adding to our drive to keep pushing against the tide."

I barely remember the bands playing that night. I was too busy checking on Danny, keeping my eye on the Elks, and making sure we abided by our time limits. At the end of the night, the Sadistic Exploits called me up to the stage to thank the audience for attending. I don't think I had ever even spoken into a microphone before, and it was an *enormous* thrill, staring out into the crowd of hundreds of faces. I yelled, "Thank you for coming! I can't believe we did it! I'll see you all back here for Punk Fest II!"

I count Punk Fest I as one of the happiest days of my life. We had pulled off a huge event effectively, and we succeeded in bringing the music to Philly's kids. I felt a tremendous sense of accomplishment.

❦

With the triumph of Punk Fest I, of course we wanted to immediately follow up with Punk Fest II while we had momentum. We set a date for later that month, December 1981. I immediately booked Decontrol again and the Proteens. "Wouldn't it be cool if we tried to bring in a bigger band?" I suggested.

"Anti-Pasti is touring," Robbie said. "How about we get them?"

We all loved the British punk band Anti-Pasti. One day at work, I made a terribly expensive overseas phone call to Anti-Pasti's management in England. I told the manager, "Look, we're a bunch of kids, and we're doing our own shows, but we're making them all-ages so anyone can come and see the band, not just those who are twenty-one. Tons of kids will be there. Our last show was a huge success and we nearly sold out."

By the end of the phone call, I had convinced the booker. Anti-Pasti was slated to play Punk Fest II. I was ecstatic! Not only were we about to promote another great punk fest, but now Sadistic Exploits would share the stage with one of our favorite bands. What's more, we were bringing an international act to Philadelphia.

Unfortunately, our excitement was short-lived. Soon, we discovered that Bobby Startup, the DJ and booker for the East Side Club, had snatched the band away from us and hired them to play his club. A few days after they had agreed to play Punk Fest II, I received a call from Anti-Pasti's management. "Hey," they said. "The band would really like to play your show, but if we turn down this East Side Club, we won't be able to book the other bands we represent at that club. I'm sorry because I like what you're

Flaunting the fortune we made doing Punk Fest. RIKKI ERCOLI

doing, but Anti-Pasti is going to have to play the East Side Club."

The Exploits and I knew little about the procedures and politics of the music industry. We were putting on shows for the sheer love of it. All we knew was that we had booked Anti-Pasti *first*. We had sought them out, we had made contact, and we were ready to get the ball rolling. We were furious at Bobby. I felt he had swooped down to mess with our all-ages show for no other reason than to squash what we were trying to do. Bobby was a good fifteen years older than us, and I felt he was out to destroy our youth movement.

We declared an open and public war. I called everyone. "Can you believe what Bobby Startup is doing?" I said, full of righteous indignation. "We booked them first!"

Lee Paris happily capitalized on the feud by having us both on his WXPN radio show, where the Exploits and I battled it out with Bobby. We explained that the East Side club could book any band it wanted, and we didn't understand why Bobby had to book the *one* band that had already agreed to play our show.

Next I called Martin Roper, the singer of Anti-Pasti, to make sure he knew what was happening. At the costly rate of about a dollar per minute for the overseas call, I thoroughly explained what Bobby had done, and I encouraged Martin to play our show. "It seems counter to what you write about and sing about," I said. "You should be playing your music for the kids!"

Martin said he wanted to play our gig, but his hands were tied. "The entire American tour is booked," he said. "I don't know if there's much we can do now."

Meanwhile, we proceeded with organizing Punk Fest II without Anti-Pasti, but we didn't give up. The battle raged on right until show time. Since my apartment was located directly above the East Side Club, we hid in the stairwell of my building and intercepted Anti-Pasti as they arrived to unload their equipment. Since our show was fairly early, and Anti-Pasti was playing late at the East Side Club, we corralled Martin and asked him, "Hey, do you want to come hang out at the Elks and see what you're missing?" He did.

So we brought Martin to Punk Fest II. He saw all the kids packed into the Elks, and he expressed enormous disappointment he wasn't playing our all-ages show. His show at the over-21 East Side Club was not nearly as well-attended. But even without Anti-Pasti, Punk Fest II was a resounding success. Having one punk fest under our belt made the second one that much easier. Once again, Danny worked the door. Peddrick was stage manager, making sure bands got their equipment on and off the stage on time. All the bands played their hearts out. The Proteens were seasoned professionals, and they set the bar high. Informed Sources were more relaxed onstage, having conquered their first-show nerves. Of course, I felt the night belonged to the Exploits, whose live performance had been perfected. Bryan was a compelling front man, often sinking to his knees as he belted out lyrics. Peddrick was a talented guitarist, and Robbie played his bass low, like Sid

Fielding phone calls about the Anti-Pasti drama on Lee Paris's
Yesterday's Now Music Today radio show on WXPN. RIKKI ERCOLI

Vicious, banging it around to the delight of fans. I knew after this night I
wanted to promote more shows.

❦

Our feud with Bobby Startup continued for a couple more years.
Eventually, we all were banned from the East Side Club for a number of
reasons—including the fact that one of the Sadistic Exploits began having a
fling with Bobby's girlfriend. One night, Killing Joke was playing at the East
Side. I really wanted to see them, but I was persona non grata. So I put on a
wig and tinted glasses and breezed right past the security guards. I even used
my VIP pass from the opening days of the club for free entry. I walked right
to the front and sat on a speaker at the edge of the stage. When the band
appeared, I whipped off my disguise. I knew the place was too crowded for
the bouncers to get to me. When the show was over, I laughed at them as I
walked out the door.

At the end of 1981, I moved about seven blocks east of the Adelphia House to a fourth-floor apartment at Ninth and Clinton. Change was in the air. Bryan and I broke up. So much had happened in the year since we met, and we were too young to take our relationship any further. It was awkward at first because I still managed the Exploits, and we were together a great deal, but we settled into an easy friendship. I began to spend a lot of time with my old crush, Johnny Vukich. He reminded me of one of my first pop star heartthrobs, David Bowie's guitarist Mick Ronson. I had always loved Johnny from afar, so being with him was a dream come true. He was sweet and fun to be around. We even got tattoos together—he got my initial N on his arm, and I got a heart and my favorite Discharge song title: "Fight Back." I always felt like I was fighting something, so it seemed appropriate.

One afternoon, Johnny and I were at my apartment, and I looked out my fourth-floor window and saw Bobby Startup walking down the sidewalk below. "Let's get him!" Johnny said.

We filled a pitcher with cold water and dumped it out the window and onto Bobby's head. I don't know if we hit him; we were too busy rolling around on the floor of my apartment laughing.

These days, I regret parts of the silly feud we had with Bobby Startup. He was a complete tool for interfering with our all-ages show, but I do respect him now for being a visionary and for his role in bringing punk to Philly. But for a brief time, he was the enemy.

10
BAD BRAINS, BLACK FLAG, AND THE BIG TAKEOVER

IN DECEMBER 1981, BLACK FLAG RELEASED ITS FIRST FULL ALBUM, *Damaged*, featuring the DC transplant Henry Garfield, now officially integrated as Henry Rollins in the L.A. band and its wild mindset. We thought the record was amazing. We reveled in clearing the dance floor when we were out wildly thrashing around and the DJ played "Rise Above" or "Six Pack." I'd wink at Allison and jokingly say, "I don't want to see anyone we don't know on this floor when that song is over." After I listened to *Damaged*, my English punk records seemed slow by comparison—well, except for the high-speed sonic wall of Discharge.

Hardcore punk truly took over in front of our eyes during the course of 1982. The days of glam and punk rock began to seem like a distant memory in the wake of bands like the scorching Bad Brains and the muscular new Henry Rollins–fronted version of Black Flag.

There's been a great deal of discussion nowadays about whether girls were ever up front or in the pit at those early hardcore shows. There are stories about guys supposedly telling their girlfriends to "hold their coats" so they could dive into the pit. Not in Philly. In Philly, women ruled shows, and we knew it.

The year began with a creative boom. On January 28, 1982, a new club called Love opened at South and Broad in Philadelphia. Promoters Chris

Bad Brains, the Elks Center, January 1982. I'm up front and in awe. KAREN KOUMJIAN

Boas and Tom Sokol wanted a place where bands and artists could hang out and share their work. They hung a big banner with the word *LOVE* stitched in colored fabric over the outside doors because they couldn't afford a real sign. Love began hosting Philly bands like Bunnydrums, Executive Slacks, the Stickmen, and the Vels, along with poets including Marty Watt. Between punk shows, Love also put on fashion shows and art exhibits.

Love had a great feeling. Sometimes young kids from the neighborhood would come inside the club and break-dance, and then pass the hat for tips. Their skills were impressive. Hip-hop and rap had merged with Philly's other forms of underground culture. The musical language of the streets and many of the neighborhoods could be heard blasting in the clubs between bands, and throughout the day coming from speakers mounted outside stores like the Sound of Market Street and Gola Electronics.

Love welcomed all genres of music and booked a colorful mix of shows. The cross-pollination of those influences created some compelling and innovative music. You could just as easily see a synthesizer "band" at Love as you could hear electro funk or hardcore punk. These kinds of music were developing all around us, and were very aware of each other.

The guys in Autistic Behavior hung out at the home of Steven Eye, who lived in an always boisterous apartment right at the tip of South Philly. Steve had a video camera—a huge, heavy monstrosity—which he lugged to shows to videotape bands. Videoing was relatively new back then; it was mind-blowing to watch shows we had attended being played back the next day. Another modern marvel was the ATM—or MAC machine, as we called it in Philly. Before the MAC machine, we had to race to the bank before it closed to cash our paychecks before going out on Friday nights. If we ran out of money over the weekend, we were flat out of luck.

After Johnny moved to the West Coast, I started to hang out at Steve's house with the ABs and met Steve's roommate Bruce Momich. Bruce had a good job—he was in the Navy. Meanwhile, he was a punk, a skater, and a graffiti artist. He was also smart, responsible, and easygoing. Since

I still worked at a law firm, it was nice to have a buddy who understood conservative job pressures. We became best friends. Bruce and I went to shows together. Almost every night we'd meet for dinner, walking down to the Gallery mall for gyros or heading over to Jim's for cheesesteaks. A lot of the time we'd just hang out at my apartment or at Bruce and Steve's place, watching videos of recent shows and talking about music.

Touring bands often stayed at Steve's house. The long-running California band True Sounds of Liberty, aka T.S.O.L., came to town and stayed there. I'd seen T.S.O.L. before, at City Gardens, when their singer, Jack Grisham, came out wearing a skirt. Jack gave zero fucks about what anyone thought, and I found that refreshing. T.S.O.L. was political, gothic, and hardcore all at the same time; I thought it was cool. And I dug the band's whole California surfer vibe. When T.S.O.L. played Love, I connected with Jack, whom I found to be hysterically funny and devastatingly handsome. We stayed up all night drinking Ortlieb's beer and walking the streets of Philly.

The ABs—especially bassist Craig Surgent and their friend Bruce Momich— constantly talked about the Bad Brains, a Black punk band from Washington, DC, who had moved to New York City. They raved about the band's musicality and intensity and said once I saw the Bad Brains, my life would change.

As it turned out, they were right. The ABs booked the Bad Brains to play with them at the Elks Center. They made an event out of the show, calling the night "The Action Ritual." The Excuses, Seeds of Terror, and Informed Sources also played. Two brothers, affectionately called Small and Tall, played in Seeds of Terror, and they'd repurposed the Dogtown skateboard logo for their band. There was something of a summer vibe about SOT even in the dead of winter, and if they were playing, I wanted to be there.

The Bad Brains show at the Elks was transformative. I have never experienced anything quite like the current coursing through my body and brain when the Bad Brains took the stage. I had always had a physical response to live music—starting when I first saw Rod Stewart, Bowie, Alice

Witnessing the Bad Brains from the front row at the Elks Center, January 1982. KAREN KOUMJIAN

Cooper, and Queen back in high school. But the Bad Brains were far more powerful.

When the band began playing, I was in the back, keeping a watchful eye on little Zeke Zagar, the thirteen-year-old son of mosaic artist Isaiah Zagar. I didn't want Zeke or his friend, Jeffrey Thies, to be stomped in the chaos. Within a few minutes, however, the magnetic pull of the band drew me all the way to the front of the stage.

The Bad Brains were extremely talented musicians. They played *so* fast and loud, but they also played *well*. Guitarist Dr. Know shot off searing riffs that pierced straight to my core. The Bad Brains' singer, H.R., was the most manic front man I had ever seen. He did backflips onstage. There was truly nothing in punk, or hardcore, or *any* genre of music like the Bad Brains. I still struggle to put into words their dynamism on stage in the early 1980s.

After that first show, I told my friends: "I'm going to see this band every single time they play, and I'll go anywhere in the tristate region to see them."

I kept that promise. My friends and I started to take road trips to every Bad Brains event in New York, New Jersey, and Pennsylvania. Their explosiveness was unsurpassed and otherworldly. I participated with sheer abandon. Sometimes the shows would last late into the night, and frequently they were on weeknights. Once after driving home from an out-of-state Bad Brains show, my friends dropped me off at the revolving doors of the PSFS building on a Thursday morning. I tried to get respectably dressed, putting my pantyhose on in the elevator, so I could work a full day.

Gradually, the Bad Brains began to add more reggae material to their sets, which I liked—as long as they still played their faster hardcore songs. When they started to embrace Rastafarianism, however, they also adopted misogynistic and homophobic attitudes, and it became harder and harder to support them. We began to hear stories about the Bad Brains making derisive and inflammatory comments about gay people and women. I was terribly conflicted during this transition because I loved their music. I just wanted them to shut up and play.

Lyrics and what bands had to say on and offstage always mattered to me. Since the time I was able to read, I pored over lyric sheets and interviews with bands in fanzines. I knew I related much more to Black Flag's "Rise Above" than I did to Crass's "Big A, Little A." The Dead Kennedys' "Nazi Punks Fuck Off" felt more relevant and immediate than Anti-Pasti's "No Government." I appreciated the education I got from song lyrics. But if bands were going to be spouting homophobic and misogynistic rants, I would not support them.

❧

One day, Sadistic Exploits' drummer, Miguel, came to practice looking like he had something to say. "I'm joining No Milk," he told us, meaning a local arty punk band led by a Bowiesque singer named Mark. "It's what I want."

All of us were a bit angry at first, until we found Howard Twiggs to replace Miguel on drums. Howard was physically imposing—the epitome of the strong, silent type. He was quietly introspective, and a very solid and powerful drummer.

In March 1982, Lee Paris organized a show with Flipper at the Elks. The neighborhood was still as dangerous as ever, and punk kids were getting jumped and mugged coming and going from shows. The cops had zero interest in the area, period, let alone in protecting a bunch of punks who they felt had no business being in the neighborhood in the first place.

For some odd reason, Lee turned for help to the Guardian Angels, a brand-new volunteer watch group who touted themselves as "unarmed crime prevention." Lee asked them to do security for the Flipper show, and they agreed. As Bruce Momich remarked, "The last thing we need is a fucking paramilitary group at one of our shows!"

Predictably, the Angels did not understand the pit. They started fights and tried to throw kids out for slam dancing. As YDI's bassist Chuck Meehan recounts, "Every time the Angels tried to toss someone out, we would circle them and form a human cocoon around the kid, so the Angels could not get to the person. It eventually boiled over, and an Angel karate-kicked [local punk] 'Tall Dave' Wynters and sent him to the hospital with a broken rib."

As a consequence, the event was a disaster. Lee was roundly criticized and castigated. At least during the Flipper show debacle, my friend John Koo played sax with Flipper on a lengthy rendition of "Sex Bomb." That was awesome.

I loved and respected Lee. I didn't like that he had called in the Guardian Angels for protection, but I didn't hold his mistake against him. When one day in May he called me and asked if I wanted to collaborate on a show, I was happy to hear from him. I knew that promoting a show would be massively less stressful if I was working with someone experienced like Lee to share the responsibility.

I had been itching to try my hand at booking bigger bands. On one hand, I was terrified about doing larger shows due to the risks involved. On the other hand, I was anxious to take our operation to the next level. After doing two punk fests, I felt I had the basic format down, and working with the Elks was pretty easy. Basically, I only needed a two-hundred-dollar deposit for the PA to get a show going.

Black Flag were arranging a tour with Saccharine Trust that would be perfect for us. At the time, bassist Chuck Dukowski booked Black Flag, and Lee called him to set up the show. I talked to Autistic Behavior about opening. The Elks were willing; the PA was secured. Now it was DIY or die.

❦

Even when I promoted a show, I always made sure to experience the event to the fullest. I needed somebody to hold *my* coat the night of Black Flag. Allison and I were smashed right up front against the stage, down a bit from drummer and badass Becky Wreck. Henry Rollins was fully in charge of the microphone for Black Flag now, bringing a more physical presence, and the band had just started to get into playing heavier, more dirgelike songs. Henry paced, screamed a lot, and at one point exchanged blows with someone in the audience.

The surviving video from that Black Flag show at Elks Center should dispel any doubt about the role of women in the Philly hardcore punk scene. You can see my white-blonde head and Allison's pink-haired head right up front. Sure, we took more than a couple of boots to our heads; we couldn't help that if we were up front under a barrage of stage divers. Years later, Allison audited the entire video and counted nine direct connections to her skull. Since I wasn't as tall as Allison, I think I absorbed a couple fewer. But it didn't matter to any of us. The intimacy of being so close to the band was worth it. We never gave it a second thought. I wasn't as tough as Allison, but I wasn't a wilting daisy, either. I guess the point is that we weren't the little women the world wanted us to be—we were just ourselves, having fun.

After the show, someone had a party at their apartment, and Black Flag came. I remember Chuck Dukowski and I talked about having the same sneakers, which were like a green Sears brand that had four stripes instead of the three like Adidas had. That's something people often forget about the salad days of hardcore—punks could switch quickly from frightening to excruciatingly nice.

❦

Throughout 1982, new Philly punk and hardcore bands were forming all the time. Every day it seemed like there was a fledgling band emerging, and we all worked to support each other. Chuck Meehan and the enigmatic Neil Perry formed YDI. YDI was a bit angrier and more aggressive than most Philly bands. I expected nothing less from Chuck and Neil. Chuck had been going to shows since he was born, and I wasn't surprised his band was intense. Neil was always the first one in the pit and the first one in the air at every show. He was a vicious front man. I was in awe of these guys and truly psyched when they started their own band. Howard Twiggs from Sadistic Exploits joined them on drums.

Little skater Zeke Zagar formed McRad with singer Ethan Jarvis, guitarist Chuck Treece, and drummer Tristan Reignier. Not surprisingly, their music was fast skate punk.

Meanwhile, the Exploits and I booked Crucial Truth, the Mob, and Public Disturbance to play at the Elks on July 3, 1982. The day before the show, my friends from New York, Jimmy G., John Watson, and Chris Charucki from Cause for Alarm all came to visit Allison and me ahead of the show. When the guys arrived at my apartment, they had a huge American flag with them. The thing was massive. I had no idea where they had gotten it. We went to Jim's Steaks for dinner, walked all over the city, and drank lots of Ortlieb's, which we called Joe's Beer because the label said "Drink Joe's Beer." Then we decided to spray-paint the entire wall of my studio apartment with band names and logos.

On Saturday morning, my little brother Danny called: "Yo, Dad and I are coming down with a present for you, so you better get those guys out of your apartment!"

The weather was oppressively hot, and my dad had decided to drive down to Philly from Norristown to surprise me with an air conditioner. I knew my dad, a Marine, would not have understood three punks from New York City visiting me in my tiny apartment, even if we were all just friends. He would freak out when he saw my spray-painted wall. I didn't know what to do. Jimmy had the brilliant idea to cover everything with the gigantic American flag, which was the exact size of the wall. It looked awesome. Since Allison was staying with me for the weekend, I told her to take our guests to lunch. I tossed her some money and begged her to get them out of my place fast.

By the time my dad arrived to install the AC, the beer cans had been tossed down the trash chute, the carpet had been vacuumed, and the place was clean and orderly. My dad loved the big American flag draped on the wall. I was so grateful for the much-needed air conditioner. I whispered thanks to Danny for having the good sense to warn me that he and my dad were coming.

Later I dragged Chris and Jimmy to the Franklin Institute, walking down to North Twentieth Street from my apartment at Ninth

New York visitors Jimmy G., Chris Charucki, and me after we had just jumped into a fountain.

and Clinton. Because of the heat, we ended up jumping into a fountain, a long-standing Philadelphia tradition. When we got home, we drank more Ortlieb's and blasted the Bad Brains ROIR cassette so loud that my neighbors banged on my door and threatened to call the police. I loved my New York pals, and when we were all together, they often made me laugh until I cried—no exaggeration.

Eventually, we headed over to the Elks for the show. Crucial Truth was still one of my favorite bands, and they and the other bands delivered energetic performances that were hot, sticky fun. Many more people from New York had come down for the event. They all tried to schmooze their way inside. I figured that if they made the trip, letting them in for free was the least I could do.

The New York bands were like the DC bands in that they always mobilized their supporters to travel to out-of-town shows. We all were rooting for one another, and it was thrilling to see everything growing bigger, week by week. Although most Philly bands could never afford to tour or play much farther away than New Jersey or New York, we always tried to support them on the road, too. To this day, though, I think the Philly bands never truly got their due mostly because they didn't tour as intensely as hardcore bands from other cities.

That December 1982, Harold Passman, the owner of Love, was shot in a robbery. Control of the venue was passed to Bart Passman, his son. Bart sought out Howard Saunders, a huge punk and hardcore fan; my friend Bruce Momich; and Steve Eye, the innovative artist, to begin booking the venue. They became Bungaboosheye Productions. At that point, hardcore punk truly took over, bringing full circle a process that had basically happened in front of our eyes over the course of 1982.

11
BOMBED AT A
DEAD KENNEDYS SHOW

EVERY WEEK I BOUGHT NEW RECORDS. My apartment was spilling over with small independent or self-released records from far and wide by bands like Chron Gen, Flux of Pink Indians, Discharge, the Exploited, and Blitz—not to mention T.S.O.L., Agent Orange, Youth Brigade, Bad Religion, the Germs, Circle Jerks, and Fear.

During the summer of 1982, I bought the first Society System Decontrol record at Third Street Jazz. Known as SS Decontrol, the band came from Boston, which had a robust hardcore scene ahead of most cities. I immediately loved that record, *The Kids Will Have Their Say*. SS Decontrol had a heavier sound, and they were formidable. They embraced the anti-drinking straight edge message championed by the DC bands, which wasn't for me, but I couldn't help but love the band.

I wanted to bring SS Decontrol to Philly. On the album insert was phone number and a message: "SS Decontrol wants to play your town." I dialed the number in an attempt to book the band a show at the Elks.

Al Barile, the band's guitarist and songwriter, answered the phone.

"My name is Nancy," I told him. "And I book shows in Philly. We do all-ages shows, and you'll make enough money to cover your expenses to make the trip." I gave him the date of our next show.

Al checked his calendar. "Well," he said, "we'd really like to play, but we have a show up here that day."

I was disappointed. Still, Al and I stayed on the phone for nearly four hours—which I regretted once my ridiculously exorbitant phone bill arrived later that month. Long-distance phone calls cost about ten dollars an hour back then, so this one cost me plenty. Time had slipped away from me. The hardcore punk scene was so small in those days. Al and I knew many of the same people across the country. We swapped stories about the bands and scenesters we knew.

More than that, Al was a really interesting guy. He seemed like he knew exactly what he wanted in life. I stayed on the line because I didn't want the conversation to end, and I think Al felt the same way. Right before we hung up, he said, "Listen, my band is going to play with the Dead Kennedys and DOA in Staten Island, New York, next weekend. Why don't you come?"

I had *no* idea how I would get to Staten Island, but without hesitation I said, "I'll be there."

After I got off the phone with Al that night, I pulled out the insert in the SS Decontrol album to scope out the picture of the band. I wanted to see the guy I had been talking to. I was a little surprised when I saw Al's photo—he was a huge, muscular guy with a shaved head. To be honest, he looked a little scary!

I needed a way to get to Staten Island with no car, no driver's license, and no idea how to find the Paramount Theater. I called Bruce Momich. "Come on," I cajoled, "let's go on an adventure! You want to see the Dead Kennedys, don't you?"

Fortunately, he did. Bruce arranged for John Smith, Autistic Behavior's singer, to drive us. The weather was blistering hot when we set off after work, none of us even sure which way to go. There was no air-conditioning in John's truck, so I hung my head out the window like a golden retriever, hoping to catch a breeze. Somehow we made it to the beautiful old art deco theater in the heart of Staten Island just in time.

I was excited to see all three bands, especially SS Decontrol. I wormed my way up to the front, left side of the stage, where Al played. Nothing could have prepared me for the sledgehammer potency of SSD. Someone wrote an article about that performance for *Savage Pink* that described SSD's set as "standing a little too close to the railroad tracks." That was an accurate assessment.

Al and I located each other right after SSD finished playing. He was as badass in person as he had been on the stage. His biceps were huge, and he had an intimidating, no-nonsense look, which I thought was cool. I remember for some reason I was smoking a cigarette. I wasn't a regular smoker, but I think I was nervous. I wanted something to do with my hands, and cigarettes were always around. A lot of punks smoked. Al looked at me like I had a gun in my hand. "Oh, you smoke?" he said.

"Not anymore," I replied, and I flicked the cigarette right into the gutter. I never smoked another cigarette after that moment.

We were only able to talk for a few minutes, however, because a huge riot exploded outside the venue. Once again, punks were fighting with neighborhood kids. Bottles and other objects flew through the air and smashed on the street around us. My friend Lazar was at the epicenter of the fight. I got separated from Al, and I knew I had to find John and Bruce before I was permanently stranded in Staten Island. This time, I wouldn't be able to catch the elevated train home. Somehow I located John's red truck and waited there, hoping he and Bruce could evade the melee.

❧

The three of us made it back to Philly early Saturday morning, and I slept until my brother arrived on the train from Norristown. Danny was staying with me overnight, and I wanted to show him a fun time in the city. Assuming they'd escaped Staten Island the night before, the Dead Kennedys were to play the Starlite Ballroom that evening with the Sic Kidz, Autistic Behavior, and Informed Sources.

Frank Blank from Informed Sources had pleaded with DKs singer Jello Biafra *not* to play the Starlite because of its rocky past. We all knew it wasn't the best or safest place for a show. I was a little scared to go back to

dead kennedys

AT THE STARLITE BALLROOM

SAT. JULY 17

(AT Kensinton & Lehigh Aves.)
TAKE THE EL TO HUNTINGTON STOP

with AUTISTIC BEHAVIOR INFORMED SOURCES & the SIC KIDZ

$7

8 PM

AN ALTERNATIVE TENTICLES PROD

Kensington after what had happened when Black Flag and S.O.A. played, but I really wanted Danny to see the Dead Kennedys. So we hopped on the el and rode to the Starlite, hoping the evening wouldn't end like the previous night's Dead Kennedys show in Staten Island.

Before the first band started, Danny and I sat on a curb in front of the club. The weather was scorching hot again, and a lot of punks were milling around outside in groups. Suddenly I noticed a car driving very slowly in our direction. After living in Center City for two years, I had gained a certain amount of street sense. I did not like the looks of that car. The thought crossed my mind that its occupants might be about to start shooting at us. Danny was in the middle of a sentence when I grabbed his hand and screamed, "Run!" I pulled him down the street, running as fast as I could.

I heard a loud explosion and then people screaming. The occupants of the car had hurled a homemade bomb—made with a stick of dynamite, ball bearings, and BB pellets—into the crowd. People ran into the street shrieking with ball bearings and BBs embedded in their legs and arms. One girl's heel and ankle were severely injured. Her blood was splattered all over the sidewalk. My friend Lenny rushed her off to the hospital.

Danny and I ran back to the relative safety of the club—which really wasn't much safety at all. In my head, I guess somehow I thought I was still going to be able to see some bands. My heart was racing. I wasn't worried about myself, but I was afraid for my eighteen-year-old brother, whom I adored. Everyone else pressed inside, and the crowd churned. The smell of sweat and testosterone filled the air. My friend Victor, one of the toughest guys I knew, pulled me aside. "Stick with me," he said. "If anybody looks at me for more than two seconds, I'm banging them out."

David Carroll, who had booked this fast-deteriorating extravaganza, set up barricades to stave off the Kensington locals, who were now amassing outside and trying to break down the doors. This situation definitely needed some punk rock, and Informed Sources began to play. Farmer Dave had replaced Brian Lee on bass. Dave Gehman wasn't a farmer, but, as Frank Blank put it, "He came from Hatfield, Pennsylvania, which was a place we'd never heard of, and we had no idea where it was. Therefore, it must have been farm country."

I had met Dave at the East Side Club, and I knew Informed Sources was looking for a bass player. I made an on-the-spot introduction, and Dave joined the band. The result was a big improvement in Informed Sources' sound. Their set at the Starlite was one of their best. While they played, there were skirmishes between punks and locals who had gotten into the show. Frank tried to stop the fighting, but he was, as he put it, "as effective as Keith Richards issuing empty threats at Altamont."

To everyone's amazement, the show continued. The Dead Kennedys eventually took the stage, and Jello Biafra surveyed the room. The windows in the Starlite were round, made to resemble portholes on a boat. Jello asked the crowd, "Ever get the feeling you're on a sinking ship?" I certainly did.

It seemed that each night my life was becoming more and more imperiled, but I was still having way too much fun to stop. Some part of me craved the excitement and the risk. I certainly felt alive. When my heart raced and adrenaline pumped, every moment seemed precious and important. When combined with the music, it was a heady cocktail.

Still, I did not have a death wish. After catching a ride home and scooting my brother back to safety, I vowed never, ever to return to Kensington. Along with not smoking, that is another pledge I have kept.

Years later, I can partially understand why the Kensington kids hated punks so much. Kensington locals were fiercely territorial, and I'm sure they felt we were an invasion that needed to be driven out. They were white and poor, and they didn't have much of value except the neighborhood they lived in and the loyalty and respect of their friends. When they felt threatened, they reacted. They wanted no one—freakish punks, especially—to colonize their turf. They had no excuse for throwing bombs at us, however, territorialism and provincialism be damned.

❦

Amazingly, the Dead Kennedys attempted a third show in the region that Sunday night, at City Gardens in neighboring Trenton, New Jersey. Bruce called me and asked if I wanted to go, and I couldn't say no. This time, I stayed out of the crowd. I found a seat on top of some equipment on the side of the stage where I could watch the show without getting bruised.

Not far into the Dead Kennedys' set, though, Chuck Meehan from YDI appeared beside me. "Hey, wanna do a stage dive?" he inquired.

"Sure." I didn't realize he meant right that second.

Before I had time to think, Chuck grabbed my hand, and we raced to the front of the stage. Chuck leapt first, wiping out half the people standing in the front. I landed solidly on my head. That stage was high, and I felt like I had done some serious damage to my skull. The pain was excruciating.

Backstage a few minutes later, I was the unhappy center of attention. Jello gave me ice for my head, but I knew I should go to a hospital. My forehead was swelling rapidly. Bruce drove me back to Philly and took me to Jefferson Hospital, where I was told I had a concussion and a hematoma. Bruce was instructed to stay with me and wake me every half hour to ensure I didn't die. He knew I'd do the same for him if the situation was reversed.

Looking at myself in the mirror the next morning, I knew I couldn't go to work. One eye was completely swollen shut, and my entire face was black and blue. I looked twice as bad as when I'd gone to work with a black eye previously. And I felt terrible. Bruce was a good friend to me that day. He stayed with me through the ordeal, brought me ice and food, and made sure I wasn't passing out or bumping into walls.

I returned to work on Tuesday with my face still a wreck. I tried to explain to my coworkers about my stage dive, but no way did that sort of thing translate to a bunch of lawyers at a staid law firm. Maybe ten years after Lollapalooza arrived, they would have thought I was "edgy," but in 1982 I was totally over the edge.

Later in the afternoon, I was called into a meeting. I thought I was going to get fired. I trembled as five of my favorite lawyers sat around a conference room table. "Sit down." They gestured toward a padded chair.

Edward spoke first. "We're terribly worried about you, Nancy. We know that your boyfriend is beating you, and we want you to know we can help you."

"All of us here will do whatever we can to assist you," Ronald nodded.

I immediately burst into tears. I didn't even have a boyfriend. Their thoughtfulness was so touching, but seeing me cry only confirmed their suspicions and made them think their assumptions had been correct. I tried to explain to them what happened in both cases to cause my injuries, but my tearful protestations fell on deaf ears. I don't think they ever truly believed me. To me, injuries came along with the territory in punk, I guess the way they do with sports. It was just part of the deal. Looking back on this moment, I am incredibly grateful for these attorneys, who stepped in and spoke up when they believed I was in danger. Especially at that time, it was a powerful and brave thing to do. I have never forgotten that.

From top: *Al Barile, Massachusetts driver's license photo, 1982;*
Me at Kelly Green's pool party, New Jersey, 1982. ALLISON SCHNACKENBERG

12 I MEET MY MATCH

EACH DAY, MORE AND MORE PEOPLE seemed to be entering the hardcore punk scene. We were already a diverse group of skateboarders, peace punks, surfers, and rabble-rousers. Some people dressed in Hawaiian shirts and madras shorts; others wore leather and spikes. No one cared, and everyone was accepted. The Philadelphia scene had also merged with a whole contingent from over the bridge in New Jersey—people like Keith Pope, Lenny Crunch, Surfer Joe, Big Mike, and the brothers, Tall and Small.

On a beautiful, hot July afternoon in 1982, my friend Kelly Green hosted a pool party at her home in New Jersey. The Exploits and Seeds of Terror were slated to play in her backyard. Allison wore a brand-new Norma Kamali bathing suit—a white ribbed tank top with a high-cut black suspender one-piece over it—that was the height of cutting-edge fashion. Punks were splashing around in the pool, eating potato salad, and cooking hamburgers and hot dogs. When it started to get dark, the Exploits began to play, but right away some yokel threw a firecracker that hit drummer Howard right in the face. He had to go to the hospital.

I was growing tired of having to survive some drama every time I wanted to see and hear the music that I loved. That night, I was angry. I took the PATCO transit train back home alone. I was sick of someone always getting hurt and ending up in the hospital.

A few days later, I picked up MDC's first album at Third Street. MDC played extremely fast, which I liked, and their lyrics had a sociopolitical bent that stuck with me. That record stayed on my turntable for a long time. When MDC toured, I was thrilled that the Exploits landed a show with them at the Girard Ballroom. The venue was basically an old bank near Broad Street in Center City. Once again, the Exploits needed a drummer; for this show, Robbie Cryptcrash from New York's Cause for Alarm filled in. He played well under the circumstances, but the Exploits could have gone a lot further if they'd been able to nail down a steady drummer.

MDC delivered a live set as fast and as furious as their record. They did not disappoint. Their tour manager was named Tammy, and I was impressed with her technical knowledge. Afterwards, MDC's singer, Dave Dictor, and the rest of the band were up for talking about everything from gay rights to racial equality. I had started to pay more attention to what was happening in the country and in the world. Dave and I shared a hatred of Ronald Reagan. The movie actor president was already expanding the size of the federal government, tripling the deficit, and adding trillions to the debt. In coming years, he would veto an anti-apartheid act, ignore AIDS, steal from the Social Security trust fund, and be caught illegally funneling arms to Iran. There was plenty to dislike about Reagan. Nearly every hardcore punk band wrote at least one song attacking him—in MDC's case that was practically every song.

During the summer of 1982, I chatted with Al Barile on the phone a few more times. I was interested in him, but I figured Boston was just too far away to bother. Then my friend Liz Chapman from New York moved to Boston to be closer to Jaime Sciarappa, the bass player from SS Decontrol. I thought she was crazy to uproot herself on a whim and move so many miles from home. She surprised me. "Come on, come with me!" she said. "We can get a place together."

"Boston is way too far away for me," I said. "New York is as far as I'll go."

The next time Al called me on the phone he mentioned that MDC would be playing soon at 2+2 in New York. "Are you going?" he asked.

I loved MDC, and immediately said yes. We made plans to meet.

"Do you remember what I look like?" I asked Al.

"Sure I do!" he said. "You look like Karen Wolek from *One Life to Live*." I wasn't dismayed by the comparison. I just thought it was funny that a big hardcore dude admitted to watching a soap opera.

I took the train to New York with Allison and Robbie of the Exploits. We walked from the station all the way down to the East Village. Al and Jaime from SSD were waiting outside of Bleecker Bob's Records. My heart jumped a little seeing Al again. Our connection had definitely been building a bit over the phone.

Al had a box of brand-new SSD shirts in his car. One said SS Decontrol across the front; the other just said SSD in big white letters. He gave me one of each design, and he asked me what I thought of them. I said, "They remind me of college fraternity Greek life shirts." I was just teasing him. I thought they were very tough and cool.

At 2+2, the opening band was a noisy mix of future Beastie Boys and Reagan Youth members called Lucifer's Imperial Heretical Knights of Schism. Over loud, disjointed music they read from a pamphlet called "What Is Rastafari?" calling out the Bad Brains for their homophobic and misogynistic attitudes. Members of the Bad Brains were in the audience and threw eggs at the band. Then former Bad Brains roadie Jerry Williams's band Bloodclot played, and they did an anti-Rasta song called "Fire Burn."

The Bad Brains, whose music I loved, but whose misogyny and homophobia I despised, were being held accountable by their fans and peers. Next up, Dave Dictor from MDC confronted Darryl Jenifer from the Bad Brains about his homophobic attitude. That was the first time I heard the Jamaican word *bumboclaat*, and when I found out what Darryl meant by that, it pissed me off. MDC may have been bold confronting the Bad Brains on their own turf, but even though MDC formed in Texas, both Dave and drummer Al Schvitz were from New York. The Bad Brains had left a mess behind in Texas by disrespecting the bombastically gay and strong band the Big Boys, defacing their property, and making misogynistic and homophobic remarks. I was glad to see Dave stand up to Darryl, even as I was also dismayed that the Bad Brains had these attitudes. They were the hardcore band I loved the most, and that had built their foundation on PMA—positive mental attitude. I found it extremely difficult to continue to enjoy their music while I was denouncing the musicians.

While MDC ripped through a frenetic set, I admit my head wasn't really in the show. Al and I stayed together the whole evening, talking and laughing. At one point, he asked me where the bathroom was. His Boston accent was so thick that I couldn't understand what he was saying. He had to repeat himself five times until he finally gave up and found it on his own. After the show, I truly hated to say goodbye.

From then on, I talked with Al on the phone almost nightly. We shared the expense of the calls, and used all sorts of ways to reverse the charges and bill the calls to other numbers. Even so, my phone bill exploded to at least two hundred dollars per month—money I definitely did not have. Al and I talked about bands and people from around the country. We both watched *General Hospital* after work—I found Al's admission of this hilarious but genuine, and we discussed the various characters on the show.

I liked that Al was painfully honest. He didn't mind admitting he watched soap operas. He liked AC/DC, Cheap Trick, and Queen as much as he liked hardcore bands. To tell the truth, so did I. Al didn't pretend to be anyone except who he was. He didn't care what anyone thought about him, his band, or his straight edge stance. For Al, straight edge was about spreading the message of choice—the choice between drinking and doing drugs and not. Al hadn't thought he had a choice when he was a kid. Finding out that you could be cool and not drink was important to him. He was the most truthful and guileless person I had ever met. Thinking about him while I was working or walking down the street made my brain swirl and my heart hurt. I was in *love*.

13
WELCOME TO BOSTON: THE KKK AND MY BABY FAR AWAY

IN AUGUST 1982, AUTISTIC BEHAVIOR AND THE PROTEENS organized an outdoor block party show on Kater Street, a few streets behind South Street. Allison and I walked to the show in the late summer afternoon heat. "Seriously." I laughed. "Could our lives be any more fun right now?"

I just loved the Proteens. Although they were quite young, they had been around a long time, relatively speaking, and they were always bursting with energy. Their set that night was perfect. When the ABs started playing, I climbed on my friend Howard's shoulders for an old-fashioned chicken fight. We slammed and acted silly. It was a warm, beautiful day, and we were just having a good time.

Suddenly, a ring of cops appeared in the dusky periphery, encircling the edge of the crowd. They clearly did not appreciate the show or the antics happening in front of the band. I didn't like the agitated looks on their faces; they seemed like they were about to pound us. No way could I let myself be arrested. I would likely lose my job, and my parents would kill me. However, the next thing I knew, the cops advanced and began throwing kids everywhere. I dove between two cars and then ran like hell back to my apartment at Ninth and Clinton, about fourteen blocks away.

My friends Allison, Robbie, and Lenny were among the many punks arrested that day. The police treated them horribly; they manhandled the

SUNDAY, OCTOBER 17, 1982

Protesters Break Up Klan Rally in Boston

A fist fight broke out before 22 robed members of the Ku Klux Klan arrived for a rally in Boston yesterday. About 1,000 protesters "charged en masse," according to a police official, when the Klansmen arrived in front of City Hall. At least 13 people were reported injured in the melee. The Klansmen were taken away in police vans for their own safety.

I thought of the KKK as a black mark in a history book. I was naïve to the fact that they still existed—until I helped face them down. In this old newspaper clip, it looks like I'm being held back from doing some damage.

women, and they pummeled the men. Allison was charged with failure to disperse and inciting a riot. Fortunately, her charges were dropped at her first hearing. Lenny was charged with disorderly conduct, inciting a riot, and assault. His lawyer told him to plead guilty, and as a result he received six months non-reportable probation. Once again, I felt extremely fortunate.

I told Al the story during our now-daily phone call. I urged him to come see for himself. "You have to come see me in Philly. It's a crazy place, but I want you to experience it."

Finally, one Friday in September, Al made the trip. I was beyond excited. He stepped off the plane from Boston carrying all his stuff in a pillowcase. I was elated as I showed him around the city. Al was a pizza connoisseur, so I took him to Sam's, one of the best pizzerias in Philadelphia. I wanted Al to love Philly as much as I did.

"I heard Minor Threat is playing in Baltimore on Saturday," Al told me while chewing a slice of pizza he was clearly enjoying. "How far is that from here?"

"Not that far, actually," I said. "Just a short Amtrak train ride." I was still a little wary of the DC kids after the brawl that they had helped incite in Kensington, but I had Minor Threat's records, and I liked them.

"I think we should go," Al said.

So as our official first date, we took the hour-long train ride to Baltimore. I was overwhelmed and amazed by how great Minor Threat was that night. They could barely play with so many kids crowding the stage to sing along. I became an instant die-hard fan. Though many faces were familiar from Philly shows, the DC kids were different on their nearly home turf—and when they weren't throwing fists. After they played, Al introduced me to Minor Threat's singer, Ian MacKaye, and he was so nice to me. He wasn't at all like the jerk I'd expected after my experiences when DC punks came to that out-of-town show.

Then, out of the blue, sure enough, the cops descended on this show, too. They mobilized in full force in front of the venue, with a helicopter circling overhead. Law enforcement simply could not understand the punk and hardcore movement. Based on our appearance, our open defiance of authority, our loud presence, and the physical nature of our music and shows, the police felt we had to be committing all sorts of crimes—even when we clearly were not.

Al and I ran back to the train station and returned to Philadelphia before anything further happened. It seemed the run to safety was a bonding ritual for punks, and Al and I had just made our relationship stronger. I breathed a sigh of relief. Once again, I was lucky to have escaped danger.

"Okay, I came to Philly," Al said at the end of our adventure. "Now you have to come to Boston."

I had never even been on a plane before. I was terribly claustrophobic, and I wasn't sure I could fly alone. Love won out, though—I made plans to see Al in October. Though he lived with his parents, he knew people who would let me stay with them. I didn't want to be an imposition, though. I insisted on getting a room for myself at the Bradford Hotel in the theater district of Boston.

The plane ride surprised me and wasn't at all what I had expected. The USAir commuter jet was tiny—like a SEPTA bus in Philly. The planes I had seen on TV had stairs and cocktail bars and pianos. I sat next to one of the heirs to the Strawbridge & Clothier department store fortune. Every few minutes, when I heard a weird sound, I'd ask him: "Is that normal?" He tried to explain what each noise and bump meant, and even if he was improvising some of his explanations, he did a good job of putting my mind at ease.

Al met me at the airport and drove me to my hotel. Then we walked over to the Boston Common, where his friends were speeding through the park on skateboards. I met Tony Perez, who played in Last Rites, and Pat Raftery and Richie Collins, who played in Negative FX. I met Andy Strachan, the guitarist in DYS; Paul Richards, who was known as "Punky"; and Jake Phelps, who later become editor of *Thrasher* skateboard magazine.

"Look up the hill," Al said, pointing to a gold-domed building in the distance. "That's the Massachusetts State House, where the cover of SS Decontrol's album *The Kids Will Have Their Say* was photographed." I was thrilled to be in the spot of that iconic photo. I wished I had a camera to take my own version of the picture.

I felt immediately at home in Boston. I liked the city's youthful vibe. Young people seemed to be everywhere—especially punks and hardcore kids. The Boston punks weren't as immediately recognizable. There wore work jackets instead of leather jackets, and Nikes instead of boots. Plenty of Boston kids came from working-class backgrounds, but just as many had parents who were authors or artists or professors. Quite a few of the "Boston" punks I met were actually from other cities, but were attending college in Boston—like Katie the Kleening Lady, who did the *Faster Than You* hardcore radio show with Negative FX's Jack "Choke" Kelly at Emerson College; and Dave Smalley, the singer for DYS, who was at Boston College.

At one point that afternoon, Jake asked, "Did you hear the Ku Klux

Klan is planning to stage a rally at Government Center tomorrow?"

I was horrified. I thought of the KKK as a black mark in a history book. I was naïve to the fact that they still existed and were spreading their message of hate. We listened to music that railed against racism and prejudice of any kind. Al said, "I think we should go and protest." I readily agreed. It was hard for me to believe the KKK would come to a northern city, and it turned my stomach.

The next day I rode Al's beach cruiser bike and he skateboarded to Government Center. We waited and waited for the hated Klan to arrive. "I don't think they're going to show up," I said.

But the KKK vans did eventually pull into the plaza near Boston City Hall, and right away the scene turned into mayhem. As the crowd surged toward the Klan interlopers, I lost Al in the chaos. The police hastened to grab the Klan members and toss them into wagons for their own protection. They had little kids with them wearing white robes and hoods, and I felt physically ill knowing someone could do that to children. A large fight broke out in front of me. I tried to help break it up, but the pandemonium was too much. I ran through the crowd until I found Al. "I need to get out of here!" I said. I felt suffocated and angry. My first impression of Boston was a bit skewered.

The next day, a picture of the fracas from Government Center appeared in the *New York Times*—and there I was smack in the center of the photo. I looked like I was about to intervene in the fight while a large, burly man held me back. I was a little worried my parents might see the photo. (I don't think they even knew I had flown to Boston.) Since they usually only read the local papers, I figured I would be safe.

The rest of that first trip was refreshingly riot-free. Al took me to Newbury Street to Newbury Comics and, of course, to Newbury Pizza. Newbury Comics was a record store and major hangout. I met DYS bassist Jonathan Anastas working there. A pretty blonde woman whom Al called

"Aimee Snake" also worked at Newbury Comics. She played bass in a band called the Young Snakes, and within a few years she would be the front person and bass player for 'Til Tuesday.

I visited Boston again that fall, and with each trip I became more attached to it. The city was home to a charismatic group of young people, including musicians, college students, skaters, artists, and punks. Plus it was so clean and "safe" compared to Philadelphia. Boston had an academic and intellectual feel that made it seem like an intriguing and fun place to live.

Al took me to meet Angie and Katie "the Kleening Lady" Goldman at their apartment on Queensberry Street in the Fenway neighborhood. The pair were integral parts of the Boston scene. Katie had her hardcore show on college radio, and she often put on shows in town. Katie and Jimmy Johnson were the founders of *Forced Exposure* magazine; Angie actually thought up the *Forced Exposure* name. When we got to the apartment, Katie was out, but Angie was there, and we clicked instantly. She and I quickly got into a huge argument with Al about guns.

Al and the rest of SSD had just been attacked at their practice space and a squad of goons had tried to steal their equipment. The other members of the band had run away, but Al held off the would-be thieves. "I'm thinking about getting a gun," Al said. "I've got to protect the equipment."

"Are you out of your mind?" Angie was shocked. "That's not what you want to do!"

"No way!" I agreed. "I don't want a gun in my life."

Both Angie and I convinced Al that a buying a gun wasn't the best idea.

A month after we met, Angie called me back at my home. "The Misfits are playing Love in Philadelphia," she explained. "We're thinking about a road trip." Now that they had a friend in Philly, she and Katie and their friend Mary wanted to take the opportunity to hang out and see an incredible band. I agreed. I told them they could stay at my apartment, as long as they didn't mind sleeping on the floor since the place was basically only one room. Of course they didn't mind.

That Misfits show at Love Hall was frenzied. The Necros opened and played one of the best sets Love had ever seen. During the Misfits' set, kids were jumping from the high balcony into the pit. The sound was brutal, and being with my new friends from Boston made it so much fun. I was thrilled to host those cool Boston women in Philadelphia—and proud my city provided them with a fierce experience.

I visited Boston a few more times. I remember on one early trip to Boston, with me on Al's bike and him on his skateboard, riding past Fenway Park as a Red Sox game let out. "Wow, this is so weird that you have a baseball stadium right in the middle of your city." I laughed. "That's sort of incomprehensible to me." Soon enough, that same Fenway neighborhood would become my home.

I love photo booths, and I coaxed Al into crowding into one with me for this shot.

14
A PHILLY PUNK
MOVES TO BOSTON

"**O**NE OF US IS GOING TO HAVE TO MOVE," Al said while we were on the phone one day. We had decided that we wanted to be together long-term.

I didn't see my job at the law firm as a "career," and Al had a good job he thoroughly enjoyed as a machinist at General Electric. So I volunteered. "I'll move. I'll come to Boston."

The Boston Crew had already embraced me, so I wasn't worried about making new friends in a strange city. Angie, Mary, and Katie were awesome. One day I got an envelope in the mail from a girl I didn't know in Boston named Jacqui. Inside was a cool photo of Al onstage and a nice letter welcoming me to the city. I couldn't believe how sweet everyone was to me. Jacqui and I soon became fast friends.

Breaking the news to my parents did not go so well. "I'm moving to Boston," I told my mother. She was furious; she hadn't even met Al. "What are you thinking?" she said. "You're going to move five hundred miles to be with a guy when you're not even engaged?"

But I had made up my mind—*I was going*.

On November 5, 1982, Minor Threat, SSD, and MDC played at Irving Plaza in New York City. The place was packed with a confluence of kids from DC, Philly, New York, and Boston. The room had a contentious and competitive undercurrent, which added to the energy.

I was hanging with the Boston guys when Howard Twiggs, whom I had driven up with, came up behind me and grabbed me playfully around the neck. Almost immediately about six Boston guys took him to the floor. I was screaming, "He's my friend! He's my friend!" Luckily, Howard just laughed it off.

Before SSD took the stage, Choke and some others from the Boston Crew grabbed the mic and did a "straight edge chant," complete with a "fall out," when all the Boston kids jumped into the audience at once. I'm not so sure the New York audience appreciated that, but it was pretty funny. In the end, the entire show was a hardcore love fest, and one of the best bills I had seen. Later, the story of the straight edge chant was mythologized, and I sensed a rift between New York and Boston brewing. Many folks in Philly still remembered the Black Flag/S.O.A. riot in Kensington and still harbored some resentment toward DC punks. There was a percolating hint of intercity rivalry just below the surface.

An early gift from Al when we began dating: His infamous hand-painted jacket that announced the arrival of The Straight Edge *everywhere he went.*

❦

As my move to Boston was rapidly approaching, no one believed I would actually leave Philadelphia. I gave my notice at work and asked for letters of recommendation from my bosses. My friends there, Tilly and Carolyn, didn't think I would actually leave after three years. "C'mon, you're not really going," they teased. "You don't even have a job or a place to live. Be serious."

Oh, I was going for sure. I had resolved to move. I planned to fly to Boston to find an apartment and a job.

"Are you going to be straight edge now?" My old boyfriend Bryan and my best friend Allison both wondered the same thing. I guess it was a fair question since I was dating one of straight edge's biggest proponents. I didn't know. Maybe I would.

Certain points of straight edge were extremely important to Al. He didn't drink or do drugs, and he despised cigarettes, but he never pushed

Al and my very comfortable mother, Millie, near Fenway in my first Boston studio apartment.

his views on me. He did imply that if I wanted to be with him, it would probably be best if I were straight edge, too, but it wasn't a *requirement*. I had had enough of drinking, and I was saddened to see what was happening with some of my friends who were involved with drugs. "You know," I thought, "being straight edge would actually be a relief." I realized that choice was definitely something welcome in my life.

I found a copy of the *Boston Globe* in Philadelphia and started my job hunt. Almost immediately, I found a listing for a word processor at an office services company. I flew up to Boston for the interview and to find an apartment. I had already used up most of my vacation days from my job for the year, so I only had one day to do everything.

My interview with Carol Lewis at JP Office Services in downtown Boston went well. I was worried that my punky white-blonde hair would turn off a prospective employer, especially in puritanical Boston. But Carol was open-minded, and my résumé and letters of recommendation impressed her. "Let me give you a tour of the office and tell you what you'd be doing," Carol suggested. By the end of the tour, she shocked me by offering me a job on the spot. "When can you start?"

The pay was ten dollars an hour—more than twenty-five dollars an hour in 2020 terms. That was *way* more than I'd been making at the law firm in Philly. I was also excited to work for a woman who owned her own business.

"The hours are eleven at night to seven in the morning," Carol explained. "And you will be the only employee working in the building at this time. Are you okay with that? Does it frighten you?"

"Absolutely not," I assured her. I had certainly experienced much worse in the punk and hardcore scene and living in downtown Philly.

My plans were going extremely well. Later that day, Jaime from SSD took me apartment hunting while Al was at work. I fell in love with the first place I saw, situated on Park Drive right next to Fenway Park. The studio apartment was much larger than the one I'd been renting in Philly. Though it cost twice as much, my new job at JP paid more than enough to cover any worries. The space was newly renovated, with a separate kitchen and dining area, a spacious central room, and hardwood floors throughout. I immediately put down a deposit.

"This is a great location," Jaime told me. "It's close to Kenmore Square, where we hang out, and Angie and Katie live right around the corner." I returned to Philly, thrilled to be able to check the box on finding a job and an apartment in Boston. A major change awaited.

Once again at the front of the stage, this time for SSD in Boston. GAIL RUSH

15

I'M NOT HOLDING YOUR COAT

MY MOM WASN'T THE ONLY ONE WITH CONCERNS about my life choices. My friends outside the punk scene were often concerned by the inherent misogynistic attitudes that they thought permeated hardcore. Hardcore was presumed to be a male-dominated genre, where women were denigrated. That was never my experience. Although males far outnumbered women in the scene, I cannot think of a single time when I was treated badly because I was a woman. In fact, the situation was probably the complete opposite—especially in Philadelphia.

I felt the hardcore guys always regarded me and my female friends with a great deal of respect. Certainly no one stood in the way of my promoting or attending shows or being up front or in the pit at shows. The hardcore guys always looked out for my friends and me. I often felt like I had twenty or thirty big brothers. They were fiercely loyal and protective.

Even after I moved to Boston—a city some mistakenly claimed treated women especially badly—I never saw any woman mistreated. I think most Boston women in that scene would agree. I heard tales about how "girls were prohibited from riding in Al's van," but I believe that had more to do with the fact that no girl actually *wanted* to be in the van with a bunch of sweaty, smelly hardcore and skater dudes.

I was never excluded, and the Boston guys immediately welcomed me into the fold. While I'm sure the experiences of other women differed, my time as a woman in punk and hardcore was totally enjoyable. Even while it was happening, I knew I was part of something unique and special.

Years later, I read in the book *Pretty in Punk* by Lauraine Leblanc about a paradox women supposedly faced in punk: "On the one hand," she wrote, "punk gave us both a place to protest all manner of constraints; on the other, the subculture put many of the same pressures on us girls as did the mainstream culture we strove to oppose."

During the years I spent in punk rock—as a fan of the music and as a manager, promoter, and writer—I never felt the same pressures I did as in mainstream culture. In the punk and hardcore world, I was accepted and respected, and as a result, I felt empowered. That empowerment caused me to act. That action led me to take chances like managing bands and promoting shows or even stage diving and slam dancing. I never felt that I needed to live up to some mainstream idea of what it meant to be a woman.

No one dictated to me how to dress or act. It was extremely liberating, especially in light of the way I'd been raised, under strict parental and Catholic school control. And my experience was grounded in the *music*. The music was always the most important part of the scene to me, and I had total and complete access to it.

In her book, Leblanc says, "Gender is problematic for punk girls in a way that it is not for punk guys because punk girls must accommodate female gender within their subcultural identities that are deliberately coded as male." I don't doubt that some women may have felt this way. I did not. I never felt that I was treading in a world that was limited to me because of my gender. I never felt that I had to change my identity because I was traversing a world that was "coded as male."

I can think of two instances when I was treated differently because of my gender. The first time was around 2004, when an author and filmmaker interviewed Al, SSD's Jaime Sciarappa, Angie, and me for a movie about the hardcore scene of the early 1980s. I was excited to be able to talk about my experiences in the Philadelphia scene, but I was basically viewed only as the wife of a hardcore pioneer. I was too confused by that treatment to really speak up and say something. When the movie was finished, I remember being disappointed that the work I considered groundbreaking in the early days of hardcore in Philadelphia—work which was orchestrated by women like Allison and me—was never mentioned. I mean, Allison developed a national reputation for the Philadelphia BYO (Better Youth Organization) by finding a performance space and promoting shows in the city for many years after I left. She was and is an icon.

Maybe the oversight had less to do with gender than the fact that the filmmaker was unaware of what was happening in Philadelphia during the early 1980s. Our movement was small compared to that of Los Angeles or DC or Boston. The director could not be expected to know every bit of minutiae from each city's scene. To his credit, I was interviewed later, and much more detail about our activities in Philadelphia was included in the second edition of his book.

As I grew older, the acknowledgment of women's role in punk and hardcore became a more important issue to me. The second time I felt treated differently due to my gender was also years after the fact. In 2013, I learned that someone was making a Pennsylvania hardcore documentary. I watched a rough trailer, encompassing the hardcore scene in the state from the early days to present, and was dismayed not to see any women. When I contacted the filmmaker to ask where the women were, he responded by saying, "Women have been interviewed. I'm not against the vagina." I knew immediately I wanted nothing to do with anyone who reduced women to their body parts. I never saw the finished movie.

Those two occasions were the only negative incidents related to gender that I personally encountered. While I am not so narrow-minded as to think that my experiences are universal, I can only tell my story. I believe I was fortunate. Not every woman felt the same. Some surely experienced discrimination, harassment, and abuse in the hardcore scene. Especially as the scene grew tremendously and devolved in the late '80s, it became hypermasculine, more violent, and intimidating, and that was heartbreaking to me.

For me, punk and hardcore enabled me to break free from the patriarchal bonds I felt at home, in school, and in my city. The scene gave me the strength to venture out of my comfort zone and attempt to master new challenges. It helped me to be the strong woman that I am today. I will always be grateful for that.

SS Decontrol at Buff Hall, November 1982. Al is mid-air; I'm pictured against the back wall here, grinning ear-to-ear—I'm in love! BRUCE RHODES

16

THE GHETTO RIDERS
& A HIT-AND-RUN:
A NIGHT AT BUFF HALL

DURING MY LAST WEEKS IN PHILLY, Allison, Ron Thatcher, a few others, and I started to work with Shawn Stern from the Better Youth Organization (BYO) in L.A. to create a BYO offshoot in Philly. I had connected with Shawn previously through long-distance phone calls, and I loved talking to him about the California punk and hardcore scene. Shawn played guitar and sang in Youth Brigade, and he was full of great ideas about advancing the scene and making it more accessible to kids. He organized shows; put out records by his band, 7 Seconds, and SNFU; and soon made a movie, *Another State of Mind*, about touring the country playing hardcore punk shows.

Shawn gave us his blessing to replicate his BYO model, and we began planning our first show. We were tired and frustrated with the growing rivalries and schisms between New York, Boston, Philly, and DC punks. We all had much more in common than our differences, and we wanted to bring everyone together in a hardcore show of unity. We decided our first show as BYO would feature bands from up and down the East Coast. We invited Crib Death and Flag of Democracy from Philly, Agnostic Front from New York, SS Decontrol from Boston, and Minor Threat from DC to play. At the time, I don't think we realized what an incredible lineup we had built. Ian

MacKaye later called it "a gathering of the tribes."

For some reason, our steady venue the Elks was unavailable—maybe they didn't want to host any more hardcore shows, given the recent problems. I know each time bands played there, the floor would move and shake. We feared one day the whole room would eventually collapse into the basement. (I think it *did* partially cave in during a Hüsker Dü show).

Allison announced that the problem was solved. "We found a great place in Camden, New Jersey, called Buff Hall. It's close to public transportation, and it's not far from Philly."

I didn't know much about Camden, except that it was a short drive across the bridge from Philly. Camden was a rough neighborhood, but everywhere was rough back then. I didn't foresee any more problems than usual, but I never visited the venue before the show.

My budding excitement boiled over when Al confirmed that SSD had that date open. "Whatever you do," he warned me, "do not bring me to a war zone." SS Decontrol had worked hard to accumulate nicer equipment than most hardcore bands; he didn't want it to get wrecked or stolen.

"Don't worry," I assured him. "Everything will be fine!"

I awaited November 20 with great anticipation. Not only would I see powerhouses SSD and Minor Threat play live again, but I'd also get to watch my buddies John Watson singing and Vinnie Stigma playing guitar with their young band Agnostic Front. Plus I'd be treated to seeing my local pals from Flag of Democracy playing for the first time.

The day of the show, Al picked me up in his black van. About eleven members of the Boston Crew were already crammed into the back. I was happy to reconnect with everyone again and to make some new friends from Boston. After the seven-hour drive, the Crew was ready to have some fun.

Driving through blighted Camden, I could tell Al was becoming apprehensive, but he didn't say anything. We passed burned-out structures, trash-filled lots, and crumbling, graffiti-covered buildings, and I started to grow uneasy myself.

Christine Elise McCarthy, me, and Ian MacKaye in Boston, June 12, 1983. I promoted this show at the Channel with SSD; while Minor Threat wasn't concerned about money, I was determined to get them what they deserved. I negotiated a guarantee of $1,250 and a bonus of $300 for 750 paying customers—the most they had ever received for a show. CYNTHIA CONNOLLY

When we arrived at the venue, I jumped right out of the van to figure out where to unload the band's equipment. Ian MacKaye from Minor Threat appeared in the driver's side window and started talking to Al. Suddenly a station wagon came careening down the street. The driver had long dreadlocks and a crazed look in his eyes. One instant later, the wagon plowed headfirst into the SSD van, clipping Ian, who was smart enough to grab the top of the van and jump, and tossing him into the air. The driver did not stop, but continued his rampage down the street and out of sight.

Meanwhile, Ian was down in the middle of the street. Some kids who had been skateboarding in front of the club ran to get his sneaker, which had blown off from the impact. Ian clearly needed to go to the hospital, and someone took him right away.

Inside his van, Al had rammed his head into the windshield. "I'm fine," he assured me, despite the blood dripping down his forehead.

The entire front end of Al's van was smashed, however—the vehicle that had hauled SSD's equipment and a dozen guys down from Boston was not drivable. Al and the crew managed to shove the wreck to the side of the road, and we unloaded all the equipment. The police came, and some kids who had chased the car and gotten the license plate number gave the cops that information.

Incredibly, when the police located the crazy-eyed driver with dreadlocks—they brought him back to the club. SSD's singer, Springa, saw him and screamed, "That's him! That's the guy!" But the driver said his car had been stolen—and then apparently returned in smashed condition to his driveway. The police seemed incredibly annoyed by the whole incident, and made it clear that coming back to testify in Camden was not something any of us would want to do.

Inside the club, I was a bit shocked to find Allison sitting at the bar, casually drinking a beer with about ten of the scariest-looking black biker dudes I had ever seen in my life. They looked like something out of a terrifying comic strip. She introduced the Ghetto Riders, a division of the Atlantic City biker club the Wheels of Soul. "They're going to do security for the show!" she said.

All day long, punk kids had been getting jumped, robbed, and beaten after arriving at the Camden train station and walking to the show. While Allison was working the door at the club, the Ghetto Riders had arrived and demanded entrance. She had little choice but to let them pass inside. As it happened, their clubhouse was right next door to Buff Hall. After meeting Allison and succumbing to her inimitable charm, they told her not to worry. They put the word out on the streets of Camden that Buff Hall was a Riders party that night. Right away, the attacks on the punk and hardcore kids stopped—a good solution to a nasty problem.

I hadn't realized that Camden was an extremely dangerous place, probably the worst I had ever seen. Even today, it still ranks among the most violent cities in the country. We were fortunate to have those bikers take control. I'm sure a hardcore show seemed extremely bizarre to them—the loud and chaotic music, the people bashing each other in the pit, the stage dives. Looking back, I appreciate how cool the Ghetto Riders were. They saved us that evening.

The Riders advised us to keep all the punks inside the venue after nightfall. "If you stay here, we can protect you," they said. When the club later became ungodly hot and sweaty, I disregarded their warning and went outside for some fresh air. Someone in the darkness hurled a D battery at me that slammed me right in the ribs. I thought for a second that I had been shot. I went back inside and stayed there.

With Ian at the hospital and the SSD van crushed, there was a great deal of debate about whether the show would happen, and whether any bands would even play. Then Ian returned to the venue with a broken toe and a fairly severe calf injury. He had a huge knot the size of a grapefruit on the back of his head, which was still bleeding. But he decreed that the show must go on.

My friend Steve Eye was videotaping the show, so I climbed up on a speaker and sat beside him. I had a feeling the pit would be particularly menacing that evening, and I wanted to be able to watch it all from a good vantage point. I also didn't want to get shot or stabbed. I was scared this night was going to end up like another Staten Island or Kensington. All my friends from Philly and New York were there, and I just wanted to have fun.

The young Philly bands played respectable, enthusiastic sets. I was excited to see Agnostic Front play because John Watson was a dear friend. I also loved Vinnie Stigma, whose Italian bravado reminded me of some of the kids from high school. John paced the stage with style and swagger, giving a commanding performance, and I knew then Agnostic Front would be a viable band with some staying power—even if John would leave within a year.

SSD took the stage and re-created the wall of power and force I had witnessed in Staten Island. Theirs was a mighty, physical set. Al was incensed. He stomped the stage and marched on people's heads, and their singer Springa pinballed and bounced off the other band members. The pit was manic, with kids crashing into each other and bodies flying everywhere. And Springa dedicated SSD's cover of the Buzzcocks' "No Reply" to "all those long-distance lovers out there," which I loved.

Incredibly, Minor Threat upped the intensity with a furious and insane set. Despite the fact that Ian started the set by saying, "I'd appreciate it if you didn't jump on my head," kids stormed the small stage to sing along with him. At one point, a local Camden woman climbed onto the stage and announced: "Today is my birthday! Happy birthday to me!" A hardcore kid promptly pushed her off stage and into the crowd, but Ian knew to make that boy apologize to avoid bringing any more Camden trouble upon us.

At one point, a kid taunted Ian for drinking a caffeinated drink. Ian was in no mood after being slammed by a car, and he took a couple jabs at the fool.

Throughout the chaos, I felt like I was witnessing something historic. Every single band played their guts out. Undoubtedly, this show was one of the best hardcore shows of all time. The energy and excitement seemed to last forever.

At the end of the evening, though, I anticipated a reckoning. I was scared to death that Al was going to kill me for booking him at Buff Hall and putting his friends and his band in danger. And there was still the matter of what to do about his van. I was at a loss—but I knew my dad would know what to do. I called him well after midnight from a phone in the Buff Hall office and told him what had happened.

"Hi Dad, I'm sorry for calling so late, but I need your help. My boyfriend from Boston played a show in Camden, and his car was hit. It's got a lot of front-end damage, and we can't drive it. I don't know what to do."

Car trouble (L–R): Al Barile, Eric Double-O, Ian MacKaye, Jaime Sciarappa.

"Tow the van here to Norristown," my dad instructed. "I'll take care of it."

This was the second time in my life my dad was incredibly cool when I needed him. I gave the key to my apartment to one of the guys in the Boston crew, and someone gave them a ride back to Philly. Al and I rode up front with the tow truck driver as he towed the van to Norristown.

At about three in the morning, we pulled up to my parents' driveway. I was terrified to have my parents meet Al for the first time under these circumstances. Among other things, Al had a shaved head, and back then *nobody* outside our scene had a shaved head. In addition, that shaved head was freshly scabbed and awful looking from hitting the van's windshield.

My mom and dad were sweet to Al, even though I could clearly tell they were a bit horrified. Al doesn't talk much if he doesn't have something to say, and he can be a little off-putting, to put it mildly. My mom gave him a glass of orange juice with ice cubes. Al eyed the ice cubes skeptically and asked, "How come you put ice cubes in orange juice?"

I was mortified. I just wanted to drop the van off and get back to my apartment in Philly as soon as possible.

While Al and my dad emptied the van, Al unloaded about six baseball bats into my parents' garage. My dad noticed them and asked, "Oh, are you all on a baseball team?" I was *dying*.

"Just leave the car with us," my parents said. "We'll take care of everything." And they did. Al got his car back a few weeks later, and it was almost as good as new—except for the steering wheel, which was put on upside down.

Al and I rode with the tow truck driver back to my apartment in Philly, where I stepped across a smelly rug of Boston boys covering every inch of the floor. Al and I ended up sleeping in the bathroom, because there wasn't anywhere else left. It was close to dawn anyway.

We all went to IHOP for breakfast the next morning. Some Boston girls met us, too, and we had so much fun strolling around Philly as a crew. First some police stopped us, and later some feds—men dressed in suits who were clearly some kind of law enforcement—who asked us what we were doing in Philly. The Boston Crew was a particularly intimidating looking bunch. But I felt like I was walking those streets with my tribe.

I still had to figure out a way for SSD and the crew to get back to Boston. I grabbed the phone book and ordered a large U-Haul truck. What I didn't realize was that I had hired a big cargo truck with no lights inside and no windows in the back. The guys had to travel in total darkness, unable to communicate with Al while he was driving, or the other kids up front. In the end, they made it back to Boston just fine.

❦

In the aftermath of Buff Hall, I was worried that Al would never speak to me, but he called me as soon as he got back to Boston—and almost every night that week. I was still scheduled to relocate to Boston at the end of December, and I couldn't wait. I just wanted us to be together.

Two days before my move to Boston, the Bad Brains were slated to headline three nights of "retirement" shows at CBGB in New York. SSD was asked to open one of the shows, along with the New York band Antidote. It didn't matter that I needed to pack up my apartment so I would be ready to move. I didn't care that the show was only a day or two after Christmas—there was no way in hell I was going to miss it.

I don't think Al believed I would make the show, but I arrived in the Bowery just in time for SSD's set. The long, filthy, narrow room was packed with clammy, sticky kids, including many of my New York friends. SSD played an intense, blistering set that was easily one of their best. They had recently added a second guitarist, which made their sound even more dense and powerful. The crowd churned and roiled in the pit, and I stayed against the side of the stage rather than risk an injury. Right before the end of SSD's set, Al did one of his trademark jumps, leaping into the air with total abandon. This time, as he hit the floor the neck of his guitar snapped right off its body. Both pieces of his beloved Gibson SG dangled around Al's neck.

In his van outside of CBGB, Al was inconsolable. "I loved that guitar," he said.

"Don't worry," I said. "We can fix it." Luckily, I was able to coax Al back inside for the Bad Brains, because that was one of the last shows where that band delivered its signature explosive, full-on hardcore assault.

I *still* watch the precious video of this performance about ten times a year. The recorded sound is dreadful, but the camera frame can barely contain the energy and explosiveness of the band and their loyal, crazed fans. I love seeing my friends in the crowd. Everyone is so young, enthusiastic, and insanely happy to be experiencing one of the best live bands that ever existed. Some of those friends have passed away, and some others I still talk to frequently. Watching that video always takes me right back into the moment.

After the show, Al said, "Just drive back to Boston with me. I don't want you to be at the train station by yourself." But I still had to prepare for my move. So he drove me to Penn Station, where I waited alone for the early morning train. I napped with one eye open to avoid the patrolling police and their nightsticks. I arrived back in Philly at about 5 a.m. Exhausted, I slept all day instead of packing.

My mother arrived to help me with what she thought were the final details, and she was dismayed at my lack of progress. "You've barely done anything!" she exclaimed.

Al would be driving down in his van to get me the following day. But my mother was an amazing packer. When we were kids, she could easily pack a small tent trailer with all the food, clothing, and supplies a family of five would need for a two-week camping trip. I told her, "I am merely deferring to your expertise."

She was not amused. She still wasn't pleased I was moving to Boston in the first place, but she was willingly helping me because she recognized my determination. She also agreed to come with me for the first week to help me get settled—and to make sure my living situation passed muster. I was fortunate my mother and I always had a loving relationship, and I'm happy to say it only grew stronger after I moved away. My mother visited me often, and I enjoyed planning our "itinerary," which could include anything from a Robert Mapplethorpe photo exhibit to seeing SSD play at a place called Spit. My mom was always up for anything, and all my friends loved her.

My longtime friends Allison and Bryan met me at my apartment the morning I left for Boston, and we said a tearful goodbye. I would miss them terribly. My three years living in Center City had been terrifying, exciting, instructive, enlightening, and so much fun. I still feel the impact of my time there. There's something about Philly that becomes part of your soul. It never leaves you, and for that, I am grateful.

That morning my mother and I, Al, Jaime, and Jaime's friend Brita helped me cram everything I owned into Al's van. What didn't fit, I left on the sidewalks of Philadelphia, along with a sizable piece of my heart.

AFTERWORD

IT'S BEEN ALMOST FORTY YEARS since these heady days of punk and hardcore, but I still think about them all the time. As a teacher these days, I continue to see the impact punk has had on me as an educator and as a person. Punk helped me be resilient during difficult times, and has enabled me to be ambitious and resourceful when I need to be. My time in Philly was transformative. I'm not grandiose enough to think that my role in the scene was anything but tiny, but I appreciate how the interconnectedness of the scene made everything work. Punk and hardcore gave me some of the happiest years of my life, and that music is a huge part of who I am.

A great deal has changed since 1982. Many of the people I loved so much are gone. My sweet and understanding mother, Millie, passed away in 2008. My dad, who could fix anything from a lawn mower to a difficult situation, died in May 2018. My first boyfriend from the high school cafeteria, Gerry, was present at the funeral. Beth Ann Lejman, Joe Stack, John Smith, Mary Ann Ghoul, Johnny Vukich, Chris Charucki, Lenny Crunch, and so many more have all left this realm. We miss them so much.

I still keep in touch with many of my old punk friends. They are the most amazing people I have ever known. We've had two reunions in Philly where, after thirty-plus years, I reconnected with Sheva, Anne, Carol, Lisa, Frank Blank, Neil Perry, Craig Surgent, Bryan, Chuck Meehan, Steve Eye, Zeke Zagar, David Roller, Lisa Mauro, Rory Miller, Joe McMenamin, Rachel O'Donnell, Maureen Walsh, Jeff Harris, Ginny Traynor, Dave

"Bass" Brown, Bill Mosko, Peter Dello Buono, Toby Reinert, Richie Cohen, Bruce Howze, David Brookman, Adam Avery, Paul Misner, Yoni Kroll, Mike Condi, Dennis McHugh, Tall Dave, Tommy Ajax, Mark Sargent, and so many others.

I feel so fortunate to have these people in my life. Charlie Carroll, for example, helped launch my school's rock ensemble. He found people to donate musical equipment for the students. My punk friends are incredible people who support me and my students' projects, motivate me, and bring a smile to my face when I need it most.

After Jaime Sciarappa from SSD moved back to Boston from California, we met for dinner. He told me he was thinking about becoming a teacher, and asked if he could observe my classes. Of course, I welcomed him. By the end of the day, he had made up his mind. I helped him begin teaching at my school. We've been friends for thirty-eight years now, and colleagues for over fifteen. If you would have told us, while we were kids standing in front of Bleecker Bob's Record Shop that we'd both be high school teachers together in the future, I don't think either of us would have believed that.

Al and I were married in 1989, and we still live in Boston. Before I moved from Philadelphia, Al did buy me a ring—a beautiful three-stone diamond ring. When my mom asked him if it was an engagement ring, he told her it was a "hello" ring. That description cracked her up—after enough time had passed. Al and I have been together for over thirty-eight years, and I think we have one of the best "how we met" stories ever.

I've tried to remember the events in this book as accurately and factually as possible, fact-checking with fanzines, news accounts, and conferring with "those who were there." Despite my best efforts, memories are fallible, and I apologize in advance for any failures in recollection.

This is just my little piece of the big story. As I said, I know other people's experiences differed, and that the same events appear different through another person's eyes. I can only tell the story of what happened from my perspective, and I'm grateful for the opportunity to do so.

Rare smiling photo of Al at our wedding, June 24, 1989.

Punk rock singalong. ALLISON SCHNACKENBERG

ACKNOWLEDGMENTS

SPECIAL THANKS to Karen Loeper for reading all my drafts, providing great feedback, and always supporting me.

Lauren Stephenson and Larissa Pienkowski, I'll be forever grateful for your skillful editing of my drafts. I can't wait until we meet in person.

Thank you, Glen E. Friedman, for rewording the title and guiding me through this process.

Rikki Ercoli, I thank you for providing so many amazing photos for this book! I'm thrilled social media has enabled us to reconnect.

There is NO way I could have remembered the intricate details of this memoir without the help of some wonderful friends. It warms my heart to know you all are there for me, some of you after thirty-eight-plus years. I am also appreciative to those of you who were part of these stories, those of you who jogged my memory, and those of you who provided photos for this book. A huge thank-you to Sheva Golkow, Chuck Meehan, Lisa Haun, and Frank Blank Moriarty for answering my relentless questions, for your continual fact-checking, and for your excellent memories.

Thanks, Jacqui Keyes, for holding my hand on a flight to DC.

I will be eternally grateful to Patti Brett, Denise Milus, Frances Rega, Mike Condi, Andrea Bono, Craig Surgent, Bruce Momich, Ian MacKaye, Bryan Lathrop, Dicky Barrett, Jack Grisham, Cindy McKitrick, Cynthia Connolly, Stephanie DiBari, Danielle LePage, Allison Schnackenberg, Vinnie Stigma, Tony Rettman, Ted Venemann, Dave Kaufman, Jason Barletta, Christine Elise McCarthy, Michael Patrick MacDonald, and Stacey Ann Finney, Gail Rush, and all the wonderful punk and hardcore kids from back in the day, who impacted my life in ways they will never know.

CAN'T WAIT 'TIL IT'S PARTY TIME

Hey, if this is the end credits, we need a playlist of theme music!

THE ANIMALS – "House of the Rising Sun" from *The Animals*

DION – "Abraham – Martin – John" from *Greatest Hits*

TOMMY JAMES & THE SHONDELLS – "Mony Mony" from *Mony Mony*

ROLLING STONES – "Paint It Black" from *Aftermath*

ROLLING STONES – "Gimme Shelter" from *Let it Bleed*

THE ARCHIES – "Sugar, Sugar" from *Everything's Archie*

THE TEMPTATIONS – "Ball of Confusion" from *Greatest Hits II*

JAMES BROWN – "Get Up" from *Sex Machine*

ROD STEWART – "Reason To Believe" from *Every Picture Tells a Story*

ALICE COOPER – "I'm Eighteen" from *Love It to Death*

ROD STEWART – "You Wear It Well" from *Never a Dull Moment*

PETER FRAMPTON – "Do You Feel Like We Do" from *Frampton Comes Alive!*

T. REX – "Telegram Sam" from *The Slider*

DAVID ESSEX – "Rock On" from *Rock On*

ROXY MUSIC – "Do the Strand" from *For Your Pleasure*

ALICE COOPER – "Elected" from *Billion Dollar Babies*

DAVID BOWIE – "The Jean Genie" from *Aladdin Sane*

RARE EARTH – "(I Know) I'm Losing You" from *Ecology*

OHIO PLAYERS – "Fire" from *Fire*

LED ZEPPELIN – "Ramble On" from *Led Zeppelin II*

BAD COMPANY – "Can't Get Enough" from *Bad Company*

DAVID BOWIE – "Sorrow" from *Pin Ups*

QUEEN – "Keep Yourself Alive" from *Queen*

LOU REED – "Sweet Jane" from *Rock 'N' Roll Animal*

KISS – "Strutter" from *Kiss*

BRIAN ENO – "Burning Airlines Give You So Much More" from *Taking Tiger Mountain (By Strategy)*

DAVID BOWIE – "Diamond Dogs" from *Diamond Dogs*

NEW YORK DOLLS – "Personality Crisis" from *New York Dolls*

AEROSMITH – "Seasons of Wither" from *Get Your Wings*

PATTI SMITH – "Gloria" from *Horses*

ROXY MUSIC – "Love Is the Drug" from *Siren*

PETER FRAMPTON – "Show Me the Way" from *Frampton*

MICK RONSON – "Play Don't Worry" from *Play Don't Worry*

THE TUBES – "White Punks on Dope" from *The Tubes*

LED ZEPPELIN – "Trampled Under Foot" from *Physical Graffiti*

DAVID BOWIE – "Sound and Vision" from *Low*

DAVID BOWIE – "Heroes" from *Heroes*

RAMONES – "Teenage Lobotomy" from *Rocket to Russia*

DEAD BOYS – "Sonic Reducer" from *Young, Loud and Snotty*

IGGY POP – "China Girl" from *The Idiot*

THE STOOGES – "Dirt" from *Fun House*

THE STOOGES – "TV Eye" from *Fun House*

THE AVENGERS – "We Are the One" from *We Are The One*

CHEAP TRICK – "Surrender" from *Heaven Tonight*

SYLVESTER – "You Make Me Feel (Mighty Real)" from *Step II*

BLONDIE – "Dreaming" from *Eat to the Beat*

PATTI SMITH – "Dancing Barefoot" from *Wave*

ELVIS COSTELLO – "Accidents will Happen" from *Armed Forces*

THE PRETENDERS – "Precious" from *Pretenders*

THE KNACK – "My Sharona" from *Get the Knack*

THE DAMNED – "Smash It Up" from *Machine Gun Etiquette*

THE CLASH – "Janie Jones" from *The Clash*

THE CLASH – "Stay Free" from *Give 'Em Enough Rope*

GENERATION X – "Your Generation" from *Generation X*

THE CLASH – "White Man in Hammersmith Palais" from *The Clash*

THE DEAD KENNEDYS – "California Über Allies" from *Fresh Fruit for Rotting Vegetables*

THE CLASH – "Clampdown" from *London Calling*

JOAN JETT – "Bad Reputation" from *Bad Reputation*

AC/DC – "Back in Black" from *Back in Black*

THE MISFITS – "Who Killed Marilyn?" from *Legacy of Brutality*

SADISTIC EXPLOITS – "Apathy" from "Freedom" b/w "Apathy"

BLACK FLAG – "Rise Above" from *Damaged*

BLACK FLAG – "Six Pack" from *Six Pack*

T.S.O.L. – "Code Blue" from *Dance With Me*

ANTI–PASTI – "No Government" from *The Last Call*

FLUX OF PINK INDIANS – "Tube Disaster"
        from *Strive To Survive Causing Least Suffering Possible*

THE DEAD KENNEDYS – "Too Drunk to Fuck" from *Fresh Fruit for Rotting Vegetables*

BAD BRAINS – "Big Takeover" from *Bad Brains*

BAD BRAINS – "Sailing On" from *Bad Brains*

BAD BRAINS – "Fearless Vampire Killers" from *Bad Brains*

MINOR THREAT – "In My Eyes" from *In My Eyes* EP

YDI – "Rizzo's Coming Back" from *A Place in the Sun/Black Dust*

AUTISTIC BEHAVIOR – "Blind Silence" from *Shattered Cattle*

KRAUT – "Unemployed" from "Unemployed" 7"

SSD – "Boiling Point" from *The Kids Will Have Their Say*

SSD – "Get It Away" from *Get it Away* EP

MINOR THREAT – "Betray" from *Out of Step*

EVELYN "CHAMPAGNE" KING – "Love Come Down" from *Get Loose*

RIKKI ERCOLI

ABOUT THE AUTHOR

NANCY BARILE has been a public high school English Language Arts teacher working with kids in Massachusetts for over twenty-six years.

In 2007, she was named a member of the *USA Today* All-Teacher Team, and in 2011 she was awarded the Massachusetts Commonwealth Award in Creative Leadership. She is a 2013 recipient of the Kennedy Center/Stephen Sondheim Inspirational Teacher Award; also in 2013 she was named Boston Red Sox Most Valuable Educator. She was a 2015 Top 50 Finalist for the Varkey Global Teacher Prize.

She is also an adjunct professor in the undergraduate and graduate schools of education of a Boston-area college. Her writing has been featured in the *Huffington Post*, *The Guardian*, *Ozy*, *Education Week*, the *College Board*, and *Hey Teach*.

Nancy lives outside Boston with her husband Al Barile and Flippy the Beagle.

Keep Reading! More from Bazillion Point

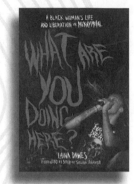

TEXAS IS THE REASON
The Mavericks of Lone Star Punk
by Pat Blashill | hardcover

WHAT ARE YOU DOING HERE?
A Black Woman's Life and
Liberation in Heavy Metal
by Laina Dawes | softcover

MISERY OBSCURA
The Photography of Eerie V
by Eerie Von | hardcover
forward by Lyle Preslar

STRAIGHT EDGE: A Clear-Headed
Hardcore Punk History
by Tony Rettman, foreword by Civ | softcover

WE GOT POWER!: Hardcore Punk Scenes From
1980s Southern California,
by David Markey & Jordan Schwartz | hardcover
w/Henry Rollins, Dez Cadena, Keith Morris, Chuck Dukows
Janet Housden, Mike Watt, Jula Bell, Joe Carducci

MURDER IN THE FRONT ROW: Shots From the Bay Area Thrash Metal Epicenter
by Harald Oimoen & Brian Lew, 292pp deluxe hardcover.

EXPERIENCING NIRVANA: Grunge in Europe, 1989 by Bruce Pavitt

NYHC: New York Hardcore 1980–1990 by Tony Rettman; foreword by Freddy Cricien

TOUCH AND GO: The Complete Hardcore Punk Zine '79-'83 by Tesco Vee and Dave Stimson

CITY BABY: City Baby: Surviving in Leather, Bristles, Studs, Punk Rock, and G.B.H by Ross Lomas

DIRTY DEEDS: My Life Inside/Outside of AC/DC by Mark Evans

HEAVY METAL MOVIES: Guitar Barbarians, Mutant Bimbos & Cult Zombies Amok!

BAZILLIONPOINTS.com | @bazillionpoints